What's It All About, Anyway?©

A Search Beyond Ourselves

by

Bruce McDougall

National Library of Canada Cataloguing in Publication
BF637.54M23 1992 158'.1 C92-091184-6

ISBN 0-9696020-0-6

Cover Design by William Stockman

Typesetting by Paul Corbin & Associates

Printed in Canada by Friesen Printers, Altona, Manitoba.

Published privately by the New Ventures Foundation
Suite 1704 - 2075 Comox Street
Vancouver, B.C. Canada V6G 1S2

Dedicated

with love
To those who taught me
and
To those I have taught
—Bruce, 1992

While the events described by 'Papa' in this book are true, names and other identifying details have been changed to protect the privacy of individuals involved.

Foreword and Acknowledgements

The motivation for writing this book was the hope that reporting some of my thoughts and experiences might assist or at least encourage others on their own search for answers, answers both on the practical aspects of life and the spiritual.

Yet, it's a paradox. The giver always receives the most. Thus I have received several gifts from writing — some expected, some unexpected. The first gift I would like to acknowledge is the warm support and encouragement that I received from so many friends. To name a few: Gerard and Shawn Grant, Paul Corbin, Marilyn Hamilton, Lucille Monette and Pat Bermel.

Secondly, I had to acquire some of the techniques of writing. This (believe it) has been quite an exercise. To the extent that I have achieved any such skill is due in large measure to the patience of Anne Curran.

Finally, re-reading what I wrote gave me quite a different viewpoint on my life. Like most of us, I'm sure, when I thought about it at all, I thought my life had been a sequential row of random experiences, a linear series of barely related events stretching from birth to old age. Now, with awe, I see it as a thing of one part, a whole, an integer of importance like a vital cog in a great machine. It's as if the atoms of my days had been ordered into structure to become the molecules of my years, and these molecules, in turn, had coalesced into the intricate pattern of a simple, multifaceted crystal. And I glimpse that my crystal, like everyone's exotic, precious crystal, fits neatly into its appointed place in the vast brilliant diadem of the cosmos.

With love, may I wish each one of you, the reader, success in your own search, that search that begins within yourself and ends far, far beyond yourself. Your success will be assured if you follow the two single rules promulgated by the Buddha 2500 years ago: Start and Keep Going.

—Bruce, 1992

Note: A condensed portion of Chapter 7 was published previously by *Reader's Digest*.

Table of Contents

Chapter 1

The Mystery

Like the hero in an ancient legend, I have heard the sacred verse, drunk the magic potion and been initiated into the mystic rites. Now, robed in shining rainment emblazoned with the secret symbols, the sword of invincibility buckled to my side, I am certain of my quest, my destiny is secure.

I smile at my fantasy. Vancouver disappears below me as my plane ascends into the clouds. What a contrast between the way I feel now and how I felt two weeks ago as my plane was descending over the city to land.

Is it really just two weeks since I arrived home? I remember wondering at the time if I could really call it home anymore, seven years after my family's move to Alburquerqui. Perhaps I shouldn't have come? Was I not risking the collapse of all my fond memories of childhood under the harsh scrutiny of maturity? I just couldn't stand more disappointment after what had happened to me over the last few weeks. And this visit with my grandfather whom I hadn't seen since I was 15. Once again, wasn't I expecting much too much? By the time the plane landed, I was sure the whole trip was a big mistake.

The airport was crowded that day —— How am I ever going to find him in this mob, I wonder. Then suddenly, I hear, "Hey, Robert," and there he is with his old familiar grin. "Hey, Papa," I yell back. As soon as we meet, ignoring my offered handshake, he enfolds me in an enthusiastic bear-hug.

As we drive into the city, Papa confesses, "I was concerned that I might not recognize you. No wonder. You must be a foot and a half taller since I saw you last.

Guess I'll have to call you Robert now and not 'Little Bub' like I used to. Little Bub sure doesn't fit you anymore, does it?"

When we arrive at his high-rise apartment, I drop my luggage at the door and immediately step out onto the patio, excited to rediscover some of the landmarks of my childhood—the freight ships of the world peacefully at anchor in the harbor, the mountains and islands blueing in the late afternoon sun, the flash of the distant lighthouse near my former home, the dark green forest of Stanley Park below, the lagoon and its fountain, Lions Gate Bridge and, in the other direction, the skyline of Vancouver.

Next I examine his half-remembered apartment, recognizing photos of myself, my parents, sisters, uncles, aunts and cousins. Then I question him about his momentos and souvenirs—the chunk of colorful crystals, the hunting knife next to the Buddha, the argellite totem pole, the Chinese gong supported by brass dragons, the paintings, the drawing of Jesus laughing in the rain. Finally I read the titles on some of his books, the books that overflow the bookcases into piles on the adjacent coffee tables and chairs.

Later, after a celebratory dinner, I confess, "I've got a lot of reasons for this visit with you, Papa. I want to see the old house where I was brought up. I want to visit some of my old friends. I want to check out the university here and see what's offered for post-graduate work. And of course, it's a vacation. I needed a break after writing my finals. And I've got a couple of personal problems as well. I needed to get away, have some time to think.

"But mostly," I continue, "I wanted to spend some time with you. When I was a kid you were so much fun — and you seemed to know everything. I remember all the things we did, even the first time you pushed me on a swing. And all your jokes and funny stories. You were a really

important person in my life, Papa. You were very special, more than just a grandparent. You used to teach me about things no one else even talked about. Mom used to say you were involved in what she called 'headstuff'. I'd like to know more about that."

"Such as—?" he prods gently.

"I feel confused right now. Everything, the whole world seems upside down. I've got to get my mind straight, try to make some sense of it all and figure out where I'm going."

Papa smiles. "It could be your age you know. I used to feel the same way when I was in my early twenties, and it's only after a lifetime of looking that I've found some answers that satisfy me. Questions such as, 'What am I here for? From whence do I come and whither go?' brought me, time and again, to face the greatest mystery of all, 'What am I?'"

"Would you tell me all about it? Start at the beginning. What got you interested in this sort of stuff in the first place?"

My grandfather smiles again, the same familiar smile. "I've never told anyone about it before," he says, and then, with a broader grin, adds, "But, on the other hand, I guess no one's ever asked me before . . .

We are the weavers of the tapestries of our lives. Each life is different; each tapestry unique, intricately designed and woven from the threads of all we have done, all we have said, all we have learned and all we have thought.

Beginning at the childhood border of my tapestry and continuing throughout its design, winds a strange golden thread which illuminates a reality far beyond the ordinary and gives a deeper meaning and spiritual significance to my life. While at times that sparkling strand has been heavily overlain by the coarser threads of the ordinary, common events of life, its continuous presence is the very warp and woof of my being, unifying the tapestry. That thread, I did not weave. Someone else was the weaver.

The identity of that unknown weaver was not revealed to me until just a few years ago. Often years passed between the events when the golden thread flashed, gleaming brightly, showing itself once more. These events, like clues in a good mystery story, seemed unrelated until the whole riddle was finally solved. The mystery began with what seems a simple, minor event.

One night in bed when I was seven years old, I saw a stranger standing in the doorway of my room. I remember that I blinked my eyes several times to make sure I was awake and not having a dream. The person seemed tall but since I was a small child lying down, perhaps he wasn't actually as tall as I thought. He was bareheaded, thin, had a small beard and was dressed in a white, flowing robe. What was most unusual, he was illuminated by a white light that shone brightly around him. A light that emanated from within him.

I felt no fear, for I sensed his love and kindness. I lay passively, feeling pleased at his visit, even honored by his presence. That's all I remember happening. Then I fell asleep.

Although I was sure he was not my father, there had been some resemblance, not just a facial likeness but also a sense of kindness. The next day I asked my father if he had come to my room that night, but he told me he had not. That seemed to be the end of that, a minor incident, soon to be forgotten and of little consequence. Little did I know. It was only the beginning, the first glimpse of the radiant mysterious strand that would wind throughout the tapestry of my life. Who was that person? Why had he been there? The mystery had started.

About this time I made the discovery of a technique which I referred to as my 'trick'. It was simple enough. All I did was repeatedly ask myself, "What am I? What am I?". After eliminating every conceivable answer as either incorrect or only partially right, I persisted with the question, "What am I?", again and again. The answers progressively came from ever deepening levels of consciousness until finally a time arrived when I could answer no more and conscious thinking ceased. Then what I referred to as a 'click' occurred. My mind stretched to 'click' into another reality and "I" seemed to rise, to be above my body so that I could observe myself and all my activities. I could see myself as I lay in bed, I could see myself getting up or getting dressed or eating. I could see myself running to school or conversing with others. My viewpoint was some 10 or 20 feet above my physical body. It was a fun thing to do. The experience would last just a short while — sometimes only for a moment, sometimes for as much as an hour — then I would be just myself again, here on earth.

As a little child I puzzled about this ability I had developed to watch myself. Although perplexed, I recognized a great truth. The 'click' experiences taught me that I was more than just my body. When I was above myself, the "I" that existed above me had no body. My body was "down there". I was seeing, but not with eyes. I was hearing, but not with ears. I reasoned that I must be a Spirit that owned or occupied a body "down there". Obviously the Spirit had some connection with this earthly body, but I, the Spirit, was part of the eternal while what happened "down there" was only during a lifetime.

At that time, I made no connection between my 'click' experiences and the glowing person who had been in my room that night. Only later in life did I occasionally ask myself, "How did I learn my 'trick'? Who was the stranger in my room? Are they clues to the same mystery?" The answer was not to unfold for another 50 years.

I could not properly describe my experience in words to anyone else because I had no words for it. Years later, I read that the Hindus call this state "witnessing". They consider that it often happens just before one is enlightened.

The one time I attempted to talk to my parents of these strange events, they laughed, not understanding what I was trying to say. Not liking to be laughed at, and not liking to be misunderstood, I decided never again to talk about such things. It was a secret I kept to myself. Even now, it takes courage to talk of these experiences which are so intimate.

For many years I continued to enjoy doing my 'trick' and assumed everyone else could do it also, even though, for some reason, they did not talk about it. I was well into my teens before I discovered that others could not. Since the teen years are a time when we greatly desire to conform to our peer group, I certainly did not want to feel strange or to appear different. I stopped performing the 'trick'.

When I tried to do it a few years later, I was unsuccessful. Although for long, long periods I posed the question, "What am I? What am I?" the 'click' did not occur. My 'trick' was lost, or so it seemed. I felt sad, believing that I had lost something very dear and precious. Now I know that it was simply misplaced. It was still there, waiting to be revealed again and again.

Of utmost importance, however — I held onto the knowledge that I was more than just a physical body. I treasured that lesson well and it has guided and helped me during crucial times in my life.

There was another lesson I learned, too, and it has carried me through all the roles which I have performed in life. I knew, beyond question, that these roles were only games I played "down there". Only my emotions, mind and body were involved in these games; my essence, my Spirit, the essential me, was uninvolved.

When I refer to my life's activities as "games", I do not mean that I was frivolous towards life and that the games of life are not important. I played life's games with great intensity, with complete concentration, and always played to improve my score. Knowing what I really was, however, allowed me to risk and to dare because the Me that is eternal could never be changed or affected by what I did "down there", on earth.

During my middle years, naturally my energies focused on being a father and provider for my growing family of four children. Richly rewarding as those life activities were, they lay like thick strands obscuring the shining thread below. Almost a quarter of a century passed before I found the next clue to the mystery. At that time I was residing in a Benedictine monastery.

For many years I went on an annual meditative retreat which lasted for forty days and forty nights, a most effective time frame. Accumulatively, I have spent well over a year in solitary meditation. My daily routine at such times included an hour for reading each evening. During my retreat at Westminster Abbey, the name of the monastery, I discovered in their extensive library a book that looked out of place on the shelf among all the heavy, black bound books on Christian religion and philosophy. That book, "Yoga", written by a Hindu called Venkatesananda, had been donated to the monks by some Eastern religious group.

The book set out to describe all the ways the author knew of meditating. The last method he described was accomplished by the meditator repeatedly asking, "What am I? What am I?" The author stated that something happened after repeating this question over and over, but he didn't know how it happened or even exactly what occurred since he, himself, had never managed to accomplish the technique successfully. He had heard that it was like climbing out on a branch of a tree and then sawing the branch off behind. Then, or so the author claimed, one experienced "witnessing", a freeing of the Spirit from the physical body.

With the joy of recognition, I yelled, "Hey — that's my trick! That's my click!" My experience of the sudden `click' was indeed comparable to the analogy of the sawed-off branch; it had left me suspended in space and free of my physical body.

The mystery was closer to solution. The next clue, found in another book, provided more answers yet.

Today, bookstores have an ample supply of books concerning spiritual matters so it is difficult to remember that it was only thirty years ago that the flower children of the "Hippie" generation created a market for them. Before that time, only a meagre selection was available to thirsty seekers such as myself.

In one of the first books printed to satisfy that new hippie demand, there was a casual reference to a Hindu Saint who had written a book with the title, "Talks with Sri Ramana Maharshi". As soon as I read the name, I felt an imperative need to find out more about him and to read what he had written. My desire was dashed when I found that the book had long been out of print. Since some bookstores have a special service, searching for out-of-print books, I contacted a dear friend who owned such a place, but to my continuing disappointment, she was unable to locate a single copy. I felt sad, heart-sick, as if an illusive, precious something of great importance had slipped from my grasp.

A few more years passed. Then, one day while browsing in a bookstore, the book, "Talks with Sri Ramana

Maharshi" seemed to leap from the shelf. It was a new edition of the old book for which I had searched years before. I opened it as soon as I was home. Inside, I found a photograph of Sri Ramana Maharshi.

Part of the mystery was solved. In my hands I held a picture of the man who had been in my bedroom fifty years before. His face and the loving kindness of his expression were familiar to me. I felt I had known and loved him all my life. No words can describe the feelings I experienced as I stared at that picture. Just looking at it gave me goose bumps. I trembled and felt like singing and crying at the same time.

Only a few facts are needed to completely cover the life of Ramana Maharshi. He was born near Madura in 1878 and died about 1950. Without spiritual training, he became enlightened as a high-school student of 17. He never left India and spent all of his adult life in the small village of Tiruvannamalai by the holy mountain Arunachala. There an Ashram grew around him.

I really had no need to read the book since I had known the essence of its contents nearly all my life. From scanning the book, I saw he referred to his teaching as "Jñana Yoga". He taught that the way of Jñana, meaning knowledge, the knowledge of what we truly are, was to incessantly ask, "What am I? What am I?" Through this technique, he explained, we could finally achieve Yoga, meaning unison, union with Divine Bliss. Jñana was my childhood 'trick'. Yoga was the 'click'.

One mystery still remained. How had I learned my 'trick'? Another book was to provide the ultimate clue and solution. In an old secondhand bookstore, I found "The Collected Works of Ramana Maharshi". This book contained his verbatim answers to questions from audiences gathered to learn from him, which question and answer sessions are called "Satsangs". Its cover was torn and stained by time, but the truth within it was timeless.

How many coincidences, how many synchronicities could I believe occurred by random chance before I would acknowledge the hand of a Master Weaver? Once more what happened was predestined. I opened the book, seemingly at random, and on the first page I glanced at, was the final solution of the whole mystery.

My eye was drawn immediately to the following question from one of his followers, "As you have the answers to the world's problems, and are able to teach the way of knowledge, why do you stay here in this small village in India? Why don't you take your wisdom to the whole world?"

Maharshi answered, "How can you assume that I only teach here and that I do not go into the world?"

In a flash I saw my whole life as a completed tapestry and the profound influence of that golden thread. The solution to the entire mystery was obvious yet seemingly impossible.

Although physically he remained in India all his life, he also taught outside India. Once upon a time, on the other side of the world, he taught a little child. He taught me.

Chapter 2

The Cup of Life

Cloudy, cool, a misty drizzle. Ignoring the weather, we walk the seawall around the park, our stride in unison. It's good to be together and beside the ocean once more. Good too is the hot chocolate that Papa makes for us on our return.

Opening the conversation, I tell him, "I've written a poem, Papa. Would you like to read it?" When he assents, I add, "It came like a vision to me all at once one morning while I was eating breakfast —— but it took me a long time to really get it right."

Glimmer

Old faces glimmer
Through the mists of time;
Beseeching eyes
Look closely into mine.

Murmurs and distant footsteps
Now draw near;
Strange hands touch mine
That strangely, once were dear.

Lost days that never were
Are lived once more
Where purple waves
Lap a shimmering shore.

In wisps of dreams
That dawn too early broke,
Deep silence whispers words
That ne'er were spoke.

Drums throb the beat
Of a different refrain;
There's a place unknown,
Where I'm home again.

Papa pours another half-cup of chocolate for each

of us. "I really like your poem, Robert," he says, putting the saucepan back on the stove.

"One other thing I must tell you, Papa. Of all those ancient faces that I saw in my vision, one face was not so ancient. That face was yours. There's so much I want to talk to you about—so much I want to learn from you. I remember some of the things you taught me when I was young—meditation for instance. I must confess though, I stopped doing it for a long time. But I started again this morning and it felt so good I wonder why I ever stopped. I also tried your 'What am I?' technique."

"Good," he encourages, "Those techniques have helped me a lot."

"Although I had a lot of questions when I came here, I now seem to have even more. For instance, as a kid, how did you handle knowing you were a spirit? You must have had problems. With no one to help, weren't you confused? What did you do? I know I would have had a hard time. You must have felt very alone. Did you feel special or important? How did you figure it all out?"

He smiles at my torrent of questions and takes a few moments to gather his memories . . .

The first questions I faced were: Why me? Why was I chosen? Was I supposed to be some messenger of God? Was I supposed to give humanity a message? If so, I sure had no idea what the message was. Or was I to be like a reporter and when I died tell God how things were going on earth? That too seemed absurd — didn't God already know everything?

Fortunately, any idea of being special did not linger, for such ideas can lead to psychotic aberrations. I came to appreciate that all of us are special for we all are spirit. The only difference was that I knew it. Even the minister at church failed to understand my questions or the significance that I *owned* my knowledge of spiritual existence. My final conclusion was that it was just no 'Big Deal'. Years later I learned that my conclusion was identical to the Buddha's for he told his disciples, "the only difference between you and me is that I remember what I am and you do not."

Further questions arose as I grew older. For instance, when I heard about saints and enlightened persons, I sometimes thought I would like to be enlightened. Other times I wondered if, perhaps, I already was. However, the saints and enlightened beings I read about all seemed to dwell in everlasting tranquility and peace and in no way was that my experience, nor has it ever been. Oh sure, I am often *at* peace, but my life has been intensely exciting. Saints, it seems, have no worldly desires. I sure as hell, or heaven, do! I enjoy good food, fine wine, travel to exotic parts of the world. I am sensuous and loving and revel in having my lover's naked body close to mine. I smoked tobacco for thirty years, consumed my full share of alcohol, made and lost money, worried and fretted, enjoyed parties and occasionally got drunk. In short, I not only enjoyed the world, but I also enjoyed myself, enjoying the world. A Saint I ain't!

Still, owning the knowledge that I am Spirit, fit the definition of an enlightened Being. So why, I wondered, didn't I act saintly? My vision of the "Cup of Life" answered this and other questions.

I had that dream when I was a teenager. A very significant dream, it remains deeply etched in my memory to this day. In my vision, I was offered a golden chalice from which to drink. It was a large vase perhaps fifteen inches high and six inches in diameter, studded with sparkling gems and of intricate design. When in my imagination I picture the Holy Grail, I see that dream goblet. It glowed not so much with light reflecting from the gold, but, rather, as if it were translucent and the brilliance came from within. It was iridescent. And very holy.

Upon closer inspection, it proved to be a dual cup, composed of two compartments or chambers. I realized I could drink as little or as much as I wished—but it was so designed that I could not avoid drinking an equal amount from each half.

I instinctively knew that one chamber contained sweet wine; the other, sour. That chalice was the two-sided Cup of Life. The sweet wine was life's joys, excitements, triumphs and loves. The other half held the bitter wine—the sadnesses, despairs, disillusionments and rejections.

I was told to consider well before I drank, since I would swallow equal portions. For every good there would be a bad; for every rapture, a depression; and for every success, a failure. Twice I was warned to consider well before I drank.

Eagerly I seized the cup in both hands and said, "I will take all of life—I will drink it all—I want everything that life has to offer me, both the bitter and the sweet." I drained the chalice and then licked the last little precious drop with my tongue.

That dream or vision came true. The contents have all been tasted: ecstatic joy and intense pain, health and sickness, failure and triumph, peace and discontent, wealth and poverty, fear, enthusiasm, boredom, excitement, hate, anger and love. In short, I've lived. And adding it all up, it has been a great experience. I'm glad I chose as I did.

I have also had, as one of the many flavors in the Cup of Life, the experience of desirelessness. During my long meditative retreats, my customary desires and wants drop away automatically. When I return to the active world, the ego desires only return slowly over a period of weeks or even months.

In my dream or vision, I now understand that I had more than two choices. Not only could I have drunk little or much, I also had the option not to drink at all. That option symbolized the repudiation of all worldly desires. That option meant living like the saints I read about, without active involvement in the world and similar to my brief experiences on meditative retreats.

One of the reasons for our existence here on Earth is "to experience"; and to experience as fully as possible—not to hide like a hermit in a cave. It is like a man who is walking slowly along life's road. A luxurious automobile stops beside him and the driver invites him to ride and be liberated from the labour of his long walk. If he accepts, the journey will be both swift and easy; there will be no dust, no striving, no struggle, no weariness. The enlightened traveller declines. He knows his destination is both safe and sure, so the ending of his journey can wait. He graciously gives thanks for the offer and explains he travels for the joy of the journey, that he has time, time to walk slowly, feeling the breeze on his skin, smelling the woods, grasses and flowers, hearing songs of birds, the chorus of frogs, the soprano of insects, seeing all the splendor and glory of creation and enjoying the exertion of his body. For him, the joys of his travel are reason enough for his journey, the journey he savours and in which he delights.

I began to understand why "I ain't no Saint." Enlightenment and liberation are not one and the same. Like the traveller in our story, one can be enlightened but not liberated.

When the Buddha became enlightened, he immediately accepted liberation as well. As a young man he had been greatly disturbed by the human suffering he saw around him. His search for enlightenment was the result of attempting to answer the question of why there was such suffering in the world. Upon enlightenment, he immediately accepted liberation, and was thereby freed from suffering. Liberated, he was free from all worldly desires and cares and lived an ascetic, reclusive life, focusing entirely on the sublime. When liberated, one loves without attachment; pities without involvement; and has compassion without touching.

Do not negate liberation, for a liberated, enlightened Being does his work, fulfills a need, and serves a destiny and purpose far beyond our common perceptions but obviously, there are two types of enlightened people:

- The first are known. They are the ones who have chosen liberation and have withdrawn far from all worldly affairs. The world knows these ascetics and reclusives for they stand apart.

- The others, the majority, are secret and unknown. They have not chosen liberation. They dwell among us and work beside us. You may meet them at the market or pass them on a busy street. Having refused liberation, they surge with the joy of life in all its glorious variety and dimensions. For these, eternity can wait.

Even the bitter parts of life have value. Had we the choice between sadness and nothing, would we not choose sadness and know that we are alive? Between anger and nothing, would we not choose anger and know that we live? Between nothing and all the bitter parts of life, would we not choose the bitter so that we can sense and revel in the fact that we are? And when our hearts break, do we not know our humanity and reach out and touch our brothers?

One additional point — the cup of life does not always mete out equal flavors. Adding up the totals, the volume of sweet wine greatly exceeds the bitter in my life. But without some bitter taste, how could we appreciate the sweet?

One final point. The cup's two sides also symbolize the spiritual and the worldly. Are we not offered a full measure of both?

Chapter 3

Weavers of Time

Rain. I leave the apartment early before Papa awakens, leaving a note that I've gone jogging. I return wet with both rain and perspiration. After a shower and change of clothing, I become lost in my thoughts and problems, and even our lunch together is practically in silence. He waits, sure that I'll talk about what's on my mind when ready.

"Papa," I begin, ending the silence, "I don't really know what to do. I have my degree in Computer Science and have a good job offer. Dad got me the offer and tells me I should take it because it's a big salary. But I'm not sure if I'm really qualified for the job. Perhaps I should do post-graduate work at the University first. But I'm not even sure if I want to spend my life doing that kind of work anyway. Guess I don't really know what I want. At university, I use to sneak away from my studies and write poetry. So maybe I should be doing something entirely different. Or maybe travel—Europe or Asia—until I find myself. How do you figure out what you're supposed to do, anyway?"

"Like you," replies the old man, sitting back in his chair, "I didn't know what I wanted as a career either. So I started a process of elimination. By taking various jobs during school breaks, I eliminated all illusions about wishing to be a storeclerk, a salesman, a civil servant, a mechanical or construction engineer, a medical doctor, and a chemist. Finally, when I got a job as a student geologist, my search was ended. Without any doubts whatsoever, I knew what I wanted to do. I've discovered too, that nothing of my early investigations for a career was wasted because everything I learned was somehow put to use later on. For success, your career should be

both exciting and one in which you are competent. I'm sure we've all heard stories like the doctor who, after ten years of specialized study found he detested practising medicine. A marriage of ability and interest is required. Finding your best choice of a career is like being at a huge smorgasbord. Sample until you find what is most delicious."

"That sounds right, but how about money? Dad says money is most important and that I should take whatever job pays best."

"Well, Robert, I've got several observations about that curious thing we call money. Seldom is wealth acquired when working for another. A salary merely provides a living. Not that there's anything wrong with that. With a living provided, other things, great things, can be accomplished. For instance, Einstein developed his General Theory of Relativity while working for a living as an obscure patent clerk. Another example: when Queen Victoria, enamored of 'Alice's Adventures in Wonderland', requested to see more of the author's writings, she was presented with 'An Elementary Treatise on Determinants' and 'A Syllabus of Algebraical Geometry', for Lewis Carroll worked for a living as a lecturer in mathematics at Oxford University.

"Beyond earning a simple living, the acquisition of a lot of money seems to follow its own rules," Papa continues. "Those whose sole motive is to become wealthy usually fail. Those few who succeed almost invariably lose it again. The rare ones I've known whose only motive was money and who managed to make it and keep it, discovered it to be a curse. They've found no happiness — alcoholism, estrangement from their wife and children, sicknesses or some other tragedy have invariably followed. The secret to acquiring wealth and keeping it is, paradoxically, to have no concern for money. Find a need and fill it. Provide a good service. Be worthwhile to

others. Strive for excellence. That is success. Wealth is not success, but it follows success, like a dog its master."

"That helps, Papa, 'cause I know I want to achieve more than just making a comfortable living. There's got to be more to life than that. How did Einstein and others do it? Is there some way, some formula, to rise above the ordinary, the conventional? How about your life, Papa? You've been successful. How did you get your start? Is there some secret, something you can tell me?"

He smiles at my usual rush of questions. . . .

When I was twenty-five I was living in a strange, remote corner of the world. I had recently arrived to work on an oil exploration crew in Colombia, South America in an area called Los Llanos, the Plains. To the north and west, the Andes abruptly towered 15,000 feet above me. To the south and east stretched the vast grassy plains, bigger than the state of Texas and at an elevation only a few hundred feet above sea level. That enormous area is drained by the Orinoco River which is over 1300 miles long and whose current dumps 50 million tons of silt into the ocean each year.

When Christopher Columbus first discovered the mouth of the Orinoco, he fantasized that this great river was the entrance to Paradise. And in fact, the river does flow into an area of great beauty, but Paradise it is not! Torrential rains flood the plains twice a year, leaching and impoverishing the hard-packed soil. Few land animals exist other than mice and various snakes — including the Giant Anacondas, boa constrictors which grow to over 75 feet in length. Occasionally I was awakened at night by the overpowering unique musky smell of snake as one of these monsters slithered near where I slept in the open.

The rivers teemed with fish, mostly edible, but with soft, watery flesh due to the fact that the river water is quite warm. A type of giant cat fish called laulao, weighing over a third of a ton could be caught. Danger also swam the rivers — flesh-eating piranha and the world's biggest crocodiles, over 20 feet in length.

When the rainy season started, the oil company I was working for decided to leave the exploration crew in the area to see if it was possible to continue working. It was not. We were trapped with our backs to the mountains, a swollen river racing half a mile in front of us and two deeply-incised raging streams on either side.

The company flew the other "foreigners" — the Americans and Canadians — to another part of the country to work. I was left in charge of the crew — the technical equipment and 80 Colombians whose Spanish I did not understand. We had nothing to do and nowhere to go. I was the only North American in a vast empty area and Villavacencio, the nearest small village, was over a hundred miles away. I was a stranger, alone in a very strange land.

One night, something happened that completely changed my life. Being near the equator, the sudden sunset plunged the world into darkness. Moonrise was some hours away. The sky was a soft, dark velvet blue out of which magnified stars shone in an array of colors — silver, red, blue and gold. An expectant hush held promises of magic. I walked to a hill some distance away from the camp and climbed on top of a large boulder which had been deposited there by an ancient glacier. In solitude I sat, listening to the ringing silence, breathing in the beauty of the night, absorbed by shadows.

Pensively, I began to look at myself, to evaluate — where was I going? — what did I want? — what were my assets, my liabilities?

First I counted my assets. On the spiritual side, recalling my childhood 'trick', I acknowledged the valuable insights I'd had. On the human, material side of life, I also had many assets. I had a loving wife and baby daughter. After wasting time by failing every other year at university,

I had a Bachelor degree in Science. I had health although my right hand was partially paralyzed, the result of an accident four years previously. And I had a job.

My liabilities seemed enormous. I had debts and could not conceive how they could ever be paid. Worse yet, the debts increased each month as my meagre salary did not cover the costs of a small apartment and food for my wife and child in Bogota, Columbia's capital. My greatest problems, however, lay inside myself. Painfully shy, I kept silent even in small groups. I was often depressed. Insecurity created a pit in my stomach. Fear, lack of confidence, prevented initiative and accomplishment. I was forced to admit I did not know where I was going. I did not know what I wanted.

Then, out of the depths of my silent contemplation, like the slow growing light of a moonrise, came a vision of the future. I remembered from my childhood revelation that my liabilities involved only the human part of my mind, emotions and body — and did not affect that part of "me" that was Spirit. That divine Spirit was connected to, and part of, the hush of the night, the rock on which I sat, the grass, the silhouetted mountain, the whole world, and even the infinity of stars, the universe itself.

While joined as one with the universe, as if I were its child, it was given to me to know that I could have anything I wished. What I mean by "it was given to me" is that I was overwhelmed by a knowing, a divine assurance, a deep certainty beyond doubting, a conviction beyond any mere wish, hope or reason.

To better understand my insight, an analogy is helpful: To weave a tapestry, we need a loom and yarn, the tool and raw material. Even more importantly we need the knowledge of how to weave, the skill. All this, however, is useless without a design, a vision of the completed tapestry, the goal. To weave the days of our life into a tapestry, we construct and size the framework of our loom, choose our model for its pattern, select the colors of our joys, the tints of our tears, the brightness of our days. We embroider our borders, design our schemes, and dream our dreams.

The revelation affirmed that I had a choice. I could choose the dimensions of my life. I could pick large, colorful and magnificent patterns or those that were small, drab and insignificant. Previously, like most of us, I had not known. I had assumed I was helpless, caught in a spider-web of events and circumstances. Now I perceived I could envision and design its very pattern. I could be what I wished to be. I could have what I wished to have. Knowing made all the difference.

With the stars of that tropical sky as witness, I resolved and determined that:

. As soon as my present work commitment had been fulfilled, I would return to my native land of Canada and establish a permanent home.

. I would be successful in my chosen field of work and devise innovations in the technology of exploration and, as the ultimate criterion of success, I would discover a new gas or oil field.

. I would establish my own exploration company and explore many parts of the world.

. I would conquer my shyness and become confident.

. I would retire at an early age. (I set my retirement goal for the age of 48. I had spent the first 23 years of my life, almost a quarter of a century, in growing up and being schooled. The next quarter of a century in my life, I decided, would be for family and career.)

. I would have as much money as I wished when I did retire;

. After I retired, I would devote the rest of my life to an inward spiritual journey.

Not only did all these plans come to pass, but everything occurred exactly within the time frame I had set. Those plans seemed impossible, as far away as the stars that night but as I look back, they were modest in comparison to the ever greater tasks that I later set myself. For instance, I discovered not one oil and gas field but several. I formed not one company but directed over two dozen. I also accomplished my goal of devising various technological innovations. One such innovation involves a rather curious experience which I'd like to tell you about.

After that night of designing my life I had more energy for I now knew where I was going. And not only my energy, but my creativity was also heightened. Shortly, I began to devise, in a unique fashion, large cross-sections of the area of earth we were exploring. By this means the great tectonic events to which the rocks had been subjected were clearly displayed and easily understood and places for accumulations of oil and gas readily depicted. This original type of cross-section presaged what later became an industry standard.

Eight years after my return from Colombia, I was in New York City in hopes of obtaining additional work for the geophysical company I had founded. I had just finished a meeting with the exploration manager of a major oil company and, as I rushed to my next appointment, I was mentally reviewing what had occurred in that discussion and planning the next meeting. I had walked rapidly past Rockefeller Centre and was waiting at the corner for a red light when a powerful feeling came over me. I sensed that I had missed something and had to go back. Ordinarily, I am extremely reluctant to ever go back because I am too eager to know what comes next. But this time the feeling was too strong to resist. I retraced my steps.

I walked back maybe two-thirds of a block and there, in Rockefeller Centre, was a large window display featuring the original work I had done a few months after that special starlit night in Los Llanos. The display by Standard Oil (now called Exxon) showed my large cross-sections. My written report was there. My maps showing where I believed there was an oil field (which had subsequently been discovered) were hanging on the walls.

So there I was in the streets of New York with a multitude of strangers passing by. I wanted to shout: "Hey, that's mine — I did that! That's my report. My writing. My drafting. My work. That's mine." But I had no one with whom to share this as the crowd flowed past.

Then suddenly, I touched a deep silence within. I was back in memory to that far distant tropical night in Colombia. So much I designed that night had already come true. Then once more I experienced a deep conviction and assurance, and knew that all other things I wanted could be mine as well. I could set more goals. I could accomplish more and live life to its fullest. Then I recalled how long I had sat that magic night until the sky had brightened at moonrise and a huge, lopsided moon had lit my solitary way back to camp.

What contrasts life holds. From my silent reverie, I came back to find myself once more on a noisy street in New York City with crowds of strangers streaming by. I joined the throng, walking as fast as I could toward my next appointment. But forever, treasured within, was the enchantment of that moment.

Chapter 4
Xanadu

I arrange to spend the day with old friends and tell Papa not to wait up for me as I've been invited to a party that night. I surprise him by returning early at 9:00 o'clock. I don't even try to hide my anger.

"Want to talk about it?" he offers.

"No!" I reply shortly, but immediately add, "I'd really looked forward to seeing my old friends. Right now I need friends. I've just broken up with my girlfriend. Guess I haven't told you about that. Anyway, it was good being with my friends to start with—talking of old times, laughing at some of the things we used to do. After that though, they only wanted to talk about their parties, the amount they drank, the drugs they'd tried. I felt excluded and recognized how far we'd grown apart."

"Thomas Wolfe said, 'we can't go home again'. We each follow our own path and paths separate, diverge. Home is a memory," Papa responds.

"Yeah, I found that out too. This afternoon I went to see our old house. I didn't knock on the door; I just stood in the yard. It felt strange. So familiar yet so different. Don't know what it was. The trees had grown, the garden was changed with different bushes and the house was stained a different colour. Small changes I'd expected, but the feeling was something else, as if I was from the past and had no right to be there now. It was sad."

Papa nods his head understandingly. "And then tonight —?"

"Oh yeah. The party! If you could call it a party," I almost shout, my anger renewed. "It was drugs and alcohol. Just drugs and alcohol. They were all doing it. Not that I haven't tried some drugs. I'm no prude. But I'm just not into that scene. I had a drink but they pushed me

to try the other stuff. Pushed me hard. After I refused they completely ignored me. I got more and more angry. I left."

"Don't blame you. I'd have done the same," he says, hoping to console me.

"Maybe I don't know what life's all about but I'm sure we're not supposed to just exist in some chemical stupor."

"Then what do you think the purpose of life is?" he asks, shifting the subject.

His diversion works. Thoughtfully I reply, "I've read a lot about Eastern religions. They say our aim should be to attain enlightenment. Do you think anyone can get it? Me, for instance?"

"Oh, of course, of course," he affirms softly.

"How? It seems to me that every religion or group not only have their own particular way but each one says their way is the only right way. How many ways do you think there are?"

"Many, many," he answers, "so many I wonder we are not all enlightened. It's as if we erected a scaffold, a framework for a mighty skyscraper. We live on that skeleton which separates us from the ground, the ground of our being. How carefully we keep our balance as we walk the beams, how diligently we hold on, how hard we grasp the false reality we've created. Surrounding us is space and light. More than the multitude of spaces between the beams of that skyscraper are the ways to fall into enlightenment."

"We fall into it? We just let go somehow?"

"So easy. So many ways," he nods.

"Like how?" I persist.

"Like meditation, for instance. It teaches us how to let go."

"I've read there are many ways to meditate. How many are there? Which is best? Why your particular way?"

Papa chuckles. "I once began making a list of all the meditating techniques I knew. I gave up after listing two dozen because there were so many more, plus all the varieties and combinations. But all techniques lead to the same destination, the same state of meditation. That is what is important. Not the vehicle that gets us there."

"What about other ways for enlightenment? Aren't drugs supposed to be one of the ways? From what I've seen, especially at that party tonight, I sure don't believe it. But maybe there are other drugs? Maybe some really are like doors to higher states? Do you know anything about it? I don't suppose you ever tried them?"

"Once I did, a long time ago."

"Once? Why just once? What happened? Would you tell me about it?"

"It began like this. . .

As I approached the table where three of my friends were sitting, I could hear Mac talking, "... so, there was this raging dragon, and it was ripping, tearing and smashing everything in its way!"

I assumed that Mac was just telling another one of his dirty jokes. I hardly expected to hear a story that would start me on a journey to a strange, far distant place. My arrival had interrupted him. "Hi! Sorry I'm late", I said, taking the last chair at the table. "Was on long distance—well report."

My friends nodded. They knew I was drilling an exploratory well in hopes of discovering oil and their nods acknowledged that a well report took priority over punctuality for our lunch engagement. Politely, they asked how things were going.

"O.K.," I answered in as neutral and noncommittal

a voice as possible, "No major problems." They asked no more for they knew that the oil industry practice was to keep results of well-drilling confidential until the owner of the well could obtain additional lands near a discovery.

Although exuberant and seething with excitement, I forced myself to relax and keep a straight face. The phone call, from the engineer at the well, had confirmed that oil had been encountered over a mile beneath the surface, just three feet from where I had calculated it would be. On test, a large quantity had flowed, assuring the firm establishment and success of my new company. It was the first well my company had ever drilled!

While questioning no further, my friends stared, hoping I might betray myself, give some sign, the slightest hint that I had made a discovery. Each managed a company engaged in petroleum exploration, the biggest poker game in the world. The cost of one bet, an exploration well, is a fortune. The odds are highly stacked against a win. On the rare occasion a new oil or gas field is found, the reward can exceed the treasure of King Solomon's mines. If they even suspected, my friends would become my aggressive competitors, scrabbling to seize some of the treasure for themselves.

I broke their inquisitive stares by glancing around the Petroleum Club's dining room, smiling and nodding to some my friends and acquaintances at nearby tables. The room itself was softly lit by chandeliers which dripped thousands of crystals. Rich, polished wall panels of mahogany reflected a soft sheen. Thick, dreary, floral carpeting reduced the hum of conversation and clinking china and cutlery to a reverent hush, while the illuminated "calendar art", which displayed the uncultured provincialism of the newly rich, added a depressing gaudiness to the place. Opulent, luxurious and ornate — attention had been lavished on every aspect of club furnishings and service, from the carefully selected vintages stored in the extensive wine cellar to the clashing colors and patterns of the marble washrooms. Everything combined in an overly elegant effect, just on the wrong side of good taste. It was — and still is — the heart of the Canadian oil industry, where executives meet, trade information and discuss deals. Hardly the locale for a story as wild and unbelievable as the one that Mac was about to tell.

Bringing my attention back to my friends and wishing partly to deflect attention from myself and partly out of courtesy to Mac, I asked him to continue with his story. "Start from the beginning," I urged. "I guess I can stand one more of your lousy stories, but only 'cause you're my friend!'

Mac grinned at my jibe, "O.K. What I was saying was how I heard of this doctor, a psychiatrist. He gives his patients LSD. Know what that is? Anyway, last week I went to his office. His wife was there, too. I swallowed these little white pills. Well! I can't describe everything that happened. Sometimes I felt huge. Other times I felt so small I thought I was going to disappear entirely. And other times, I had feelings I can't even describe. The biggest deal, though, was this dragon. It was a huge dinosaur, a Tyrannosaurus Rex, the most vicious of all those giant reptiles. I knew how it felt and thought. My God! I knew what it was like to be such a thing. I *was* that monster! I charged through swamp and jungle, ripping, clawing, uprooting and smashing everything in my way, killing and devouring in great bloody gulps. The strange thing was, I wasn't exactly that awful creature. It was more like I was its *hunger*. A greedy, furious craving that could never by satisfied. A jealous hunger to possess and devour all things, and to destroy in rage what it could not possess. I was the hunger that drove the monster to its madness. I forced it to do what it did. I ruled it. I possessed it. I was its hunger!"

We were silent as Mac finished. He looked in turn at each of us around the table hoping for understanding. The two other men at the table were obviously embarrassed. Talking about feelings was something oil company executives just didn't do. One friend nervously rearranged his napkin and stared at his hands. The other pretended involvement with stirring his drink and lighting a cigarette.

"Whew! What a thing to experience," I exclaimed before the silence could become more embarrassing. "How did you feel afterwards, after it was all over?"

Mac, relieved by my question, stated he felt good, that the experience had given him an insight into himself and that he had determined to make major changes in his life.

I was so intrigued by Mac's dramatic and fascinating experience that I even forgot the excitement of my oil discovery! I couldn't miss a wild adventure like that, I decided, and later that same afternoon made an appointment with the doctor. Three days later I was on my way to his office wondering what I had got myself into.

This was 1962, long before the drug excesses of a few had aroused lawmakers to declare LSD illegal. I was intrigued by what I'd read about it. I felt that society had grown conservative, stuffy and materialistic during the 1950's, while technology and resources had largely become focused on the production of ever more gadgets and toys. I was fascinated by how quickly the so-called hippie movement had appeared after the discovery of LSD, and empathized with the flower children. Although psychedelic drugs might ruin a few lives, I hoped they would awaken society to magic and wonder, and the world would be saved — saved from boredom, if nothing else.

The drug I took that day consisted of several pills of LSD and mescaline. Both the doctor and his wife devoted the entire afternoon and early evening to watching over me. They played an assortment of music while I "tripped out". Drug experiences have been described often enough so I will not detail all of my individual experience. However, some of the things that happened were unique and the 'trip' ultimately led me into new areas and adventures in my life.

Shortly after swallowing the pills, my vision altered, became finer, for everything I saw had an added dimension. Normally we perceive the three dimensions of length, breadth and depth. The additional or fourth dimension was a vibrating thickness as if every object were alive. Perhaps the beauty of that dimension was the vibration of molecules or the energy of atoms. Perhaps it was something else, a distant further reality. Later I would recognize, when next I saw a Vincent Van Gogh painting, that he saw as I saw. His wavy jiggly lines were no expression of insanity but were the incredibly skillful portrayal on two-dimensional canvas of the four dimensions he actually saw.

Somewhat later in my LSD experience I was "out of my body." Closing my eyes, I saw fireworks of color, bursting, exploding, as if the whole cosmos was being born anew. The effervescence diminished, then disappeared. No awareness or feelings of my body remained. It was left far behind as I drifted into space. I floated through the solar system. And then beyond that, I travelled. I wandered throughout the galaxy and drifted further still. Galaxies upon galaxies passed by and still I continued until ultimately the entire cosmos with all its multitudinous galaxies were behind me and I could view the full panorama of creation as one. I was consumed with awe and reverence at its magnificence.

Then, ever outward, yet further I travelled. I became aware of other whole universes. Each one differed. A descriptive label—'Planes of Reality'—came to mind. The cosmos I had left was but one of an infinite number of universes. On some of these planes of reality was a world similar to the one I had left, but each differed from the other in at least some vital respects. On some planes, no such world as ours even existed. On others, 'our world' was more or less distorted. All planes, however, co-existed as a whole, for creation was a unity. (My experience, remember, was before modern Physics theorized about multiple universes which, under the Quantum Theory, is today considered a real possibility, at least mathematically.)

Finally I began to wonder how I would find my way back, although it did not seem to matter greatly whether I actually came back or not. Casually I thought it might be good to return and complete my life as a human on earth. To centre myself I opened my eyes and took pictures of my family from my wallet.

Closing my eyes again, I continued to drift among the marvellous 'Planes of Reality'. I decided I wanted to return to a plane with a slight difference from the one I had left. I desired a 'Plane of Reality' where a deadend ultra-conservative society was being shaken, where life existed in frothy turmoil and man was gaining more awareness and greater consciousness and rediscovering magic. Slowly I came back to here and now, but my here and now, this 'Plane of Reality' seems a much more exciting place than the one I left.

Are there an infinite number of planes? Are there other me's on these other planes? Perhaps an infinite number? How many me's feel, think and act the same? What subtle differences are there between us? If one of the me's that had taken LSD that day was left on another Plane, how am I doing there?

After the experience was over, I had two lingering concerns. The first was an undefined misgiving, a vague feeling that the whole experience somehow had been wrong, that it was just not the way things were supposed to be. The second was a sense that the experience was still unfinished or incomplete and that there was much more to be learnt. In spite of these feelings, I nevertheless knew that I had hit a 'home run', for I had achieved a spiritual insight into creation, which was the elusive experience sought by mystics as well as the 'acid heads' who constituted the drug culture of the day.

Resolution of these vague concerns and misgivings came in time. The first — my impression that something was not quite right about the whole thing — was explained when I found a Hindu legend or parable in a book. India, with its eternal fascination with higher states of consciousness, seems to have tried everything and studied every possibility of achieving it, including drugs. A few centuries ago, drug usage became popular in India and societies of drug cults arose. However they were later discarded as a path to enlightenment, and the following parable illustrates why.

The Thief of Xanadu

Once upon a time, in a far distant land, lived a mighty King. Within his vast domain was Xanadu, a magical place of mountains, streams and wild flowering gardens. There the king built his palace with glowing towers fashioned with crystal jewels from caves of ice. When it was finished, he decreed that a magnificent celebration and ball take place to which all the nobles of the land were invited.

Near Xanadu lived a thief who, upon hearing about the great ball, determined to sneak into the palace and steal what he could. So, on the appropriate night, while the servants were busy greeting and caring for the honored guests, the thief climbed over the high stone wall surrounding the palace and stealthily crossed the magnificent gardens. He was oblivious to the beauty of the large beds of flowers or the graciousness of the tall oaks, so intent was he on avoiding being caught and punished.

Finally he reached the palace and climbed up an ivy-covered trellis from where he reached an upper window. Forcing the window open, he entered, crossed a dark room and followed a corridor to a staircase. Then he went partly down the darkened stairs until he could see the great hall below where the ball was taking place.

He observed the guests bedecked in all their dazzling jewels and finery as they danced with skill and grace to the ethereal, sublime music of a great orchestra. He heard their laughter, the joy of their delight. He saw the tables heaped with lovingly prepared foods and fine vintage wines. And suddenly he wished he could stay.

He wished that he had been invited to attend as a guest and share the pleasures, but realized he would have to sneak away into the night since he was a thief and had no right to be there. He did not belong.

Xanadu, the palace, represents paradise or nirvana and the nobles are those who have achieved enlightenment. The thief is one who only glimpses the glory of enlightenment through the use of drugs. The drug taker sneaks his way to stolen visions of paradise, but he cannot remain because he has not earned his right to be there, he has not *achieved* enlightenment. He may glimpse the rapture and glory but that is all. He has to return to the darkness from whence he came.

This fable not only answered why I had intuitively felt the drug experience was wrong but it also made me realize why, even though the experience had been fascinating, I would never wish to use such drugs again. Any method that allows one to see a further reality serves a useful purpose if it starts us on our spiritual journey but psychedelic drugs present much risk. And like the thief, when the effects of the drugs wear off, we must always "come down" and paradise fades. As the ancient Hindus found, drugs are not a shortcut to nirvana; there are more sure paths to a perpetual "high".

One of my concerns about my drug trip had now been explained. I was the thief in the story.

Beyond Xanadu

The second misgiving or concern was not as simply resolved. That vague, nagging sense of the incompleteness of the experience, and the conviction that there had been much more to have and learn persisted. To find an answer I read every book I could locate on meditation, enlightenment and esoteric teachings. Finally I discovered this 'Diamond Sutra':

When one stands before the Void
Filled with awe and wonder,
It is not enough.

While providing no solution, this sutra neatly summarized my quandary. It was what I felt about my LSD experience. But why was my experience not enough? Why, when I finally encountered the magnificence and splendor of the Void was it so unsatisfactory, so incomplete?

The sutra had given my questioning a clarity it had lacked until then. Now, when I met someone—a teacher, lecturer or religious person whom I hoped might be able to help resolve my dilemma—I would recite the sutra and ask why it was true. I felt driven to obtain the answer. It became an obsession. However, the only replies I received were startled expressions or mumbles of "I don't know", followed by very abrupt departures. In spite of these rebuffs and embarrassments, I persisted. I had to know.

After many months had passed, I heard there was a small Zen Buddhist group in San Francisco gathered around a Japanese Roshi, or Master. Hoping the Roshi could give me an understanding of the sutra, which came from the Japanese Zen tradition, I travelled to San Francisco at the earliest opportunity.

I arrived on a cold, gloomy, wintery afternoon and after checking into a small hotel, took a taxi to the Zen Institute. The Institute occupied a large, decaying wooden structure which had once been a Synagogue. A charming, bright-eyed girl was helpful and explained that although the Roshi was ill with flu and would see no one until he recovered, she could make an appointment for the next afternoon for me to see the Senshi (teacher) who was the Roshi's assistant. Furthermore, I was invited to attend a meeting that evening when the Senshi would be lecturing.

By evening there was light fog and an icy drizzle. I walked to the Zen Centre and what a depressing walk it was, past windowless unpainted warehouses, then along streets where houses seemed to be shut into themselves and whose few windows shone reluctantly with a meagre, unfriendly light. I was relieved to arrive even though its welcome lacked warmth, for the place was unheated and freezingly cold.

Inside the auditorium, about two dozen young people sat in the front pews. Only the front of the auditorium was reasonably well lit. There was a slightly raised platform holding a scuffed lectern and two chairs whose stuffing was peeking through. The sides and back of the church were dim and I felt that within the shadows lurked the ghosts of ancient Jewish Patriarches disapproving of the meeting that was about to commence.

The girl to whom I had talked that afternoon sat in the front row. Turning, she smiled and waved to me where I sat in isolation, huddled within my coat against the raw coldness. Finally a small Japanese man dressed in dark peasant garb and accompanied by two young, neatly dressed American men appeared from a door beyond the platform. They all seemed to be chattering at once. Reaching the lectern, the Senshi — for I assumed it was him — stopped while his companions took their seats in the pews.

When he first spoke I understood nothing he said. His very limited English vocabulary was lost in a heavy accent. Often he reverted to Japanese, asking the audience to help him with the right English words. His lecture thus proceeded slowly, as interruptions were frequent and often one member or another of the audience interrupted to explain the correct pronunciation of this or that word. The Senshi would invariably giggle, repeating the word several times with a slightly less heavy accent each time before continuing cheerfully with his talk.

I became aware that the Senshi's smiling face radiated an inner joy. Also, I realized that his laughter was not from any embarrassment at his shortcomings in English, but, rather, that any excuse was enough for his bubbling laughter to burst forth. My heart warmed towards him and I grew excited at the prospect of our meeting on the morrow. As my ear slowly became more attuned to his accent, I began to understand his words.

The lecture was on obtaining enlightenment. Of necessity, his points were few and simple. Now, when he laughed, I laughed. The small group up front laughed, and surely, the ghosts of the Jewish Patriarches at least had to be smiling. What had commenced as a cold, uninteresting evening ended as a very warm and memorable experience. On my return to my hotel, I slept well, feeling that my quest for an answer would not be in vain.

Arriving a little early for my appointment with the Senshi the following afternoon, I was guided to an upstairs room. It was furnished sparsely; a low Japanese tea table, an empty flower vase, a few pillows on the floor, a small framed spray of stone flowers on the wall. I stood alone, waiting. Very shortly the Senshi arrived and indicated that I should sit on a pillow beside the table. Smiling all the while, he informed me that his wife would serve tea.

His wife then appeared, dressed in her simple Japanese peasant clothes. Smiling, bowing and then kneeling beside the table, she spread the tea utensils. In silence but with much smiling and bowing to each other, the three of us then enjoyed the ceremony of tea sipped from small earthen cups. With more smiling and with a renewed attack of bowing, the ceremony ended, the utensils were gathered and the woman left silently.

"I saw you last night at Seshin", the Senshi said by way of starting a conversation.

I explained, slowly so he would understand me, that I had come from Canada and that I had enjoyed the previous evening. Casual conversation continued until he abruptly said, "You have a question". This was a statement, not a query.

I recited the Sutra that had obsessed me for so many months.

When one stands before the Void
Filled with awe and wonder,
It is not enough.

I added, "Although to perceive and experience the Void and the Nothingness is wonderful, I do not understand the Sutra. Witnessing the Void is certainly not enough, but why is it not enough?"

Raising his voice, he said sharply, "The Void is not empty!"

Surprised, I answered, "Oh, of course not!"

Looking with great intensity into my eyes, he smiled and then giggled his infectious giggle. He laughed louder. I responded in kind.

I suddenly *knew* he had experienced what I had

experienced; I *knew* he knew what I was talking about. We both knew the fullness of the Void, that place of "no-thingness". It was as if our minds were joined as one. I laughed with both the joy of sharing and in relief at finally communicating with someone who understood.

Our laughter intensified for I knew he knew. He knew I knew he knew. I knew he knew I knew he knew. And each time, as our layers of knowing deepened, the humor heightened. We laughed and laughed, holding our stomachs while tears streamed down our faces. It was insane, glorious.

Eventually, gasping for breath, we regained some composure, often broken by renewed fits of laughter. Finally, having dried my face which was wet with tears and after taking several deep breaths, I was able to speak.

"So, now please tell me, why standing in awe before the Void is not enough"

"One must not just stand there. One must go into it!"

That simple answer stunned me as if I'd been hit on the head with a baseball bat. I do not remember leaving, but I trust habit made me polite in my leave-taking. As if drunk, I stumbled down the stairs, along the streets to the ocean, collapsing weakly to sit on some pilings by the water. I sat there while my brain swam. Once more I was beyond the world and the galaxies. I floated in space and experienced the splendor of the Void. At last, I understood. Answers are so apparent once we know them but so obscure before. Of course! I had to go further into the magnificence, to experience more and more, to go deeper and deeper, further and further and further yet. It was mine to have—but not with drugs. It was mine to have but not as a stranger or a thief who stole his way there. I determined to arrive like a beloved son, welcomed Home.

Chapter 5
Prayer

A cloudless, calm day. The perfect day to go fishing. Within an hour, after packing food and drink and driving to Horseshoe Bay, our lines are in the water. The sea gently swells and sinks, the sun glittering off a million mirrors. The day warms. The monotonous purr of the motor fades from consciousness. An eagle circles overhead. A harbor seal solemnly observes our passing. Casual conversation ceases. We day-dream. Time passes.

Our reverie is suddenly shattered. Strike! The Coho twists high into the air. I've not forgotten the skill I learned so long ago and play the salmon until eventually it's landed.

When we resume fishing, the excitement has shattered our former mood. We have a need to talk, to communicate—about the fish, about the scenery, about the weather. Finally, after the excitement abates, I state, "I've been thinking about what you said last night. I want to know more."

"We all do," he smiles. "But what is it you wish to know more about?"

"Spiritual things. Spiritual techniques. You've taught me meditation and your 'What am I' technique, but how about others?"

"Such as ——?"

"Well, what about prayer, for instance? That's spiritual, isn't it? Does praying really work? Is there a proper way to do it?"

"I trust my answer will be more satisfactory than the answer I received when I asked the same question several years ago." He grins at the memory and then explains. . . .

A Minister who was a member of a discussion group

I attended, stated that his prayers were always answered. He claimed that, no matter how small or insignificant his request, it was always granted, and always immediately! Wanting to discover this great secret, I engaged in the following frustrating conversation. . .

"Please, teach me how to pray," I asked.

"Everyone knows how to pray," he replied. "There's nothing to it."

"Well, I don't always get what I want nor do I get things when I want them, so, obviously, I don't know how to pray," I stated.

"Perhaps you don't have enough faith," he suggested.

"You may be right. So teach me how to have faith."

"You can't be taught how to have faith; faith is given by grace."

"So, teach me how to get grace," I persisted.

"Grace can't be taught — it's a gift from Almighty God."

"Then, how does one obtain the gift of grace from God?"

"Only through prayer," he answered.

Laughing to myself, I asked once more, "So please, teach me how to pray!"

Life itself, not a Minister, was my teacher. My understanding came about in this way. As you may know, my daughter, your Aunt Dee, contracted Polio when she was six years old. Naturally I became sick with worry since, at that time, 1952, there was no remedy or cure. Polio was epidemic and many were dying. As each slow day progressed, the paralysis continued to spread through her body. My wife and I consulted several doctors but none could help. We were frantic, and tried anything and everything that might be of assistance. We discovered there were several research centers in various parts of the world that were attempting to find a cure. We phoned all these places but were informed that, as yet, they had not succeeded. All our efforts proved futile. Ultimately we discovered we could do nothing except hope and pray.

The paralysis continued to spread until finally our child was completely immobilized. Only her eyes could move. How pleadingly she looked to me for help. How powerless I was to do anything except tell her I loved her.

I prayed again and again, but without any apparent result. Our days of anguish dragged on. Then the day came when the doctors informed us that the paralysis, still spreading, was about to reach her heart. If it did, she would die. The crisis was expected within 24 hours.

In an agony of desperation, I again prayed. This time, something different happened. In silent prayer, I found myself saying, "There is nothing else I can do. My efforts are useless". I prayed, accepting that she should be saved only if it was God's will. Then I seemed somehow to open and fall into a very deep state of silence or peace. I still had my heartache but it seemed far away. A transcendent peace filled and surrounded me.

Suddenly, from that silence came not a verbal answer, but the sure conviction that my daughter would survive. My prayer had been answered. From despair, I was filled with joy and thanksgiving. Tears from the release of worry ran down my face. I wanted to shout. I told my wife that we could stop worrying. Of course we had more anxious moments, but that certain conviction never diminished.

Early the next morning, the hospital telephoned to inform us that the crisis had passed and that our child would live. Although the doctors said that she would probably never be able to get out of bed again, I knew she would. Although they said she would be crippled for life, I knew she would be made whole, to run and jump with joy. She is now a Registered Nurse, helping others to regain their health and thus repays the Universe.

Can we learn about prayer from my experience? Let's go into it. The dictionary says that prayer is a devout supplication, an entreaty, a solemn request. More simply, it is a communication from man to God, usually a request for something. For effective prayer there are eight rules. I'd like to share them with you.

Rule One—Silence

Prayer is effective when we go into a deep state of silence and is quite ineffective unless this deep state is reached. Praying aloud and in public achieves few results. Jesus instructed, "When you pray, go into your closet alone." The state of deep silence is where we surrender our will to a higher source and our Spirit resonates in harmony with the Great Spirit.

When my daughter was dying, I prayed as Jesus did when he said, "Thy will, not mine, be done." This was His act of surrender. It was also mine. Surrender and deep profound silence are the same thing. There we have no ego that thinks it controls. There the all-knowing, ever-present, infinitely powerful Spirit takes charge and does its work. There, our will eliminated, we get out of our own way. There we let go. There we let God.

Rule Two—Forgiveness

This subject is so important that I'd like to discuss it in detail at a later time. However, it is revelant to prayer and a comment is pertinent at this point. Our angers, hates, resentments, and regrets block the flow of power and interfere with our attempts to achieve silence within. In short, forgiveness is a prime necessity before prayer works.

When we forgive, who do we free? The one

forgiven may not be aware he is forgiven. When we forgive, we take the load from our own shoulders and free ourselves. So,

forgive the person who triggered the negative feelings originally.

forgive yourself for the harm you did yourself by treasuring your hate so long.

forgive yourself - everyone else has, long ago.

Rule Three—The Now

Always pray for what you need NOW, for instance, my need for immediate help to save my daughter's life.

At the 'Mad Tea Party' when Alice in Wonderland asks for some jam, she is crossly informed, "We have jam yesterday and we have jam tomorrow but we never have jam today!" In contrast to Wonderland's tasty jams, our 'jams' are what jams our progress in life. Yesterday's 'jams' are our regrets, our should have's, ought to have's, and intended to's. Tomorrows 'jams' are our fears, our "what will happen if's, maybe's and perhaps". Too often we regret our yesterdays and fear our tomorrows. Lost in the eternities of past and future, we lose all our nows, the incredibly precious moments of our days.

Yet we only have our todays and our needs for today. Jesus prayed to be given this day our *Daily* bread—not yesterday's stale bread nor tomorrow's unbaked dough. He also instructed us to "Give no thought for the morrow"—don't cross the bridge until you come to it. Stay in the 'now'.

Rule Four—Ask and Act

When we lack something in our life, do we lack simply because we have not asked for it? Have we bothered to pray for it? Do we really *want* it?

To have our prayers answered, we must want with

all our strength, with all our heart and with all our mind. Too often, prayer is but a casual shopping list of things we would like to have. God is not a heavenly supermarket! God is not a spiritual bellhop!

Three answers to prayers are possible: Yes, Not right now, and No. If the answer is 'No', undoubtedly there are factors in your request which you have not considered or are unknown to you. As everything in the universe interacts with everything else, the number of factors is infinite. Who, for instance, can predict the shapes of tomorrow's clouds? Perhaps we may accurately predict there will be clouds in tomorrow's sky. But how can we know the multitudes of factors that form and shape each cloud and change it from moment to moment?

Recognize that the answer is 'No' when you continuously encounter barriers and insurmountable difficulties. When this happens, look for an acceptable alternative. Invariably your revised goal will be better in every way. To continue exhausting yourself against barriers is simply foolish. God knows best how the world unfolds and what constitutes your maximum good.

If the answer to your prayer appears to be 'Not Yet', be comforted by the fact that there is a Divine Order to the universe, and that Time also needs to be filled. In this case, the only realistic attitude is to have patience.

Usually, the answer is 'Yes!' for the universe is designed to give you what you want but, like a chemical reaction, two ingredients or agents are needed before anything occurs. These two ingredients are formulated in an ancient Latin saying which roughly translates:

"Without God, we cannot,

Without us, God will not!"

A similar saying is:

Pray, believing God alone can do it.

Act, as if you alone can do it."

Our older traditional churches have emphasized one half of the formula: work hard, obey the Commandments, be a good, loyal servant, do good to others. The promised reward for all our hard work is a heaven after we die.

In contrast, the other half of the formula has been emphasized by the so-called New Thought churches: as we and the universe are one spirit, all we have to do is tell that spirit what we want and we'll get it, right now. When it doesn't work, we are accused of not believing hard enough.

Both parts, both ingredients of the formula are necessary before prayers are answered. The universe is a participating universe. We are a necessary ingredient. We must remember how to claim God's gifts. We have been given feet to take us to it, hands to reach for it, a body to labour for it and a mind to calculate and unravel complexities. We are part of the answer. We participate in making it happen.

Others, myself among them, sometimes forget half of the formula. We are the doers who feel confident we can do, achieve, discover and obtain by ourselves. We need to be reminded again and again that the little ego can do nothing and only the Spirit acting through the mind, body and emotions can accomplish anything. Like a wind that moves the waters to express waves, so a prayer is the wind that moves the Spirit to express our requests.

Rule Five—Be Specific - Visualize

Be specific about what you want, because you may receive what you *have* asked for. Be explicit and include all the specifications and don't complain if you receive what you requested, and it isn't what you really wanted.

You may pray, "Please, let me have a good-paying job," and later regret that your new job is uninteresting, boring and has potential neither for learning nor promotion — although it pays a good salary, the only request you made. Being detailed in your request allows you to visualize exactly the object of your desire. Unless you know exactly what you want, don't be surprised when the Universe doesn't seem to know either.

A young friend told me that she had prayed for an apartment of her own, away from an unhappy living situation with her older brother's wife. But her prayers went unanswered and she was unable to locate a satisfactory place. When I asked where she wanted the apartment to be, she replied, "It doesn't matter! I just want an apartment."

I prodded for a more exact answer based on her maximum comfort and convenience. "Within five blocks of where I work would be nice," she finally admitted.

"How big do you want it?" I probed further, demanding exact details.

Again, the answer, "It doesn't really matter. Even a little place would be heavenly." Again, I insisted on a more specific reply. It turned out that she really wanted her apartment to be about 800 square feet, including a well lit second bedroom for her hobbies.

I prodded for more specifics: what type of building she would like to have her apartment in, what rent she was prepared to pay, what floor in the building she preferred to be on, how modern the suite, and even what color of rugs and paint on the walls. With each question she was forced to be more and more precise until she visualized her apartment in every smallest detail. I asked her then to picture herself in her new apartment, smelling it, feeling it, and washing, dressing, sleeping, cooking, eating and entertaining in it. "Now imagine. How do you feel in your new apartment?" I asked her. "Just wonderful. I feel free—away from the domination of my sister-in-law. I feel really grown-up!"

With the process of a specific detailed visualization completed, I suggested she pray once again, clearly holding in her mind all her explicit specifications. The result was no surprise to me, although she was sure a miracle had occurred. The following day she signed a lease for the exact apartment she had visualized. It was three blocks from her work, on the third floor of an new apartment block. It was 800 square feet in size. It contained two bedrooms and the requested blue color rug. The monthly rent was on the low side of what she was prepared to pay. Even the walls were the precise off-white tone she had requested. Only after being very specific and visualizing her exact desires in minute detail was her 'miracle' able to manifest.

Rule Six—Be Confident

In prayer we may encounter a very personal presence, generally described as a loving Mother or Father. That presence is fully accepting of us and is not some vengeful, cruel judge to whom we are strangers or poor miserable creatures despised for our weakness. We are God's dear children whom He (She) loves. And we can be confident in our prayers, knowing that the "Loving Mother-Father" will naturally give what his/her beloved children ask for.

Before you were even aware of them, your needs are known. Already they are granted in essence on the spiritual plane. Our actions and prayers allow them to manifest, to be expressed on this material plane.

It is written, "Ask and it shall be given . . . knock and a door shall be opened . . . seek and ye shall find." But more than this,

When you ask, know that it already has been given.
When you knock, know that door has never been closed.

When you seek, know that it has never been lost.

Ask — it is already yours.

For the Universal Spirit, nothing is impossible. Even if our request seems unrealistic, a higher order of reality can be brought into play which over-rides the so-called normal laws of nature. Are answers to prayers miracles? The rising sun and the colors of the sunset are daily miracles. The laws of Nature are miracles. That we are not alone and in chaos is a miracle. The Creator has offered His creation to us, for our use and enjoyment. And we are co-creators with God for through prayer and action, we also have the power to create. This is the eternal miracle.

Spirit is infinite and inexhaustible. It surrounds, fills and is everything. It waits, wanting and anxious to form, express and manifest. According to Isaiah in the Bible, God instructed us to "Command thou Me!" The meaning is clear. Our prayers are the designs whereby the Spirit expresses Itself through us.

Rule Seven—The Great Needs

Jesus talked about prayer more than any other spiritual teacher. When He was asked how we should pray, He gave us the Lord's Prayer as an example. As we analyze this prayer, we find that everything asked for is intangible, save one. That one tangible item is our daily bread, which we need for survival itself. When we contemplate what else is really important to us, we discover that only the invisible, intangible things are the really important great needs in our lives: friendships, hope, trust, peace, love. Without these things, we cannot live, we are not human.

So, pray for the meaningful, intangible things of life, for all that is life-supporting, progressive and evolutionary. The beautiful prayer of St. Francis is a very tender example:

PRAYER OF ST. FRANCIS OF ASSISI

Lord, make me an instrument of Thy peace,
Where there is hatred, let me sow love,
Where there is injury, pardon,
Where there is doubt, faith,
Where there is despair, hope,
Where there is darkness, light, and
Where there is sadness, joy.

Oh Divine Master, grant that I may not so much seek
To be consoled as to console,
To be understood as understand,
To be loved as to love,
For it is in giving that we receive.
It is in pardoning that we are pardoned, and
It is in dying that we are born to eternal life.

Ultimately, there is only one thing that is really worthwhile to pray for. The inspiration for the following prayer to illustrate this point came from "An Invocation" by the Sufi, Sheikh Abdullah Ansari of Herat.

I pray Thee not for power, nor for health,
I beg Thee not for glory, nor for wealth,
I humbly ask what neither Prince nor King dare ask,
I beg Thee, Lord, give me Thyself!

Rule Eight—Praise

We can take the analysis of prayer one final step further. Because our needs are known and already granted, is there anything left to pray *for*? Should not our prayers become praise, a joyful thanksgiving, an exuberant gratitude for the wonders of all our blessings?

And when we praise, how light our burdens; how insignificant our problems; how good life is; how magnificent!

Chapter 6

The Awesome Power Unleashed

Tired and sunburnt after our day on the ocean, it's good to just sit around and have a quiet evening. I'm feeling proud about catching the salmon and very relaxced. More relaxed than I've been in a long, long time. Pensively, I say, "What you told me about prayer today was sure interesting, Papa, and I'd never heard before how my Aunt Dee's life was saved. I've read about things like that, but when it happens in your own family! —— tell me about other times when your prayers were answered? For instance, what was the most spectacular?"

"I'll tell you about one incident although describing the indescribable won't be easy. . . .

It was late August. Early fall had arrived in the Alberta Foothills. The world had turned to flame. The amber grain had been harvested and the stubble, an incandescent carpet of gold, stretched over the hills. The poplars, alders and birch trees shimmered, burning brightly in the breeze. To the West, in the high mountains, the tamaracks had become flaming torches of bronze silhouetted against the dark pines while the lower bushes, like embers, glowed red.

I had made plans to go on one of my longer meditation retreats. As my wife was not accompanying me, I felt it was very important to share a special tender time with her before leaving, to soften the pain of our parting. I picked a day in advance and prayed the weather would be perfect for a walk up Johnson's Canyon in the mountains of Banff National Park, a very special place for us. I visualized that we would have a lovely autumn day with the sun warming our backs, Johnson's creek splashing softly in the background, the waterfalls forming rainbows and showering diamonds of sparkling spray in the sun's rays, and the whole scene vibrating with the brilliance of the frost painted leaves.

The weather up to then had been superb but when our special day arrived, clouds were black against the distant mountains. Ignoring the warning of the troubled sky and firmly holding a picture of Johnson's Canyon in warmth and sunshine in my mind, we proceeded with our plans and commenced our 75 mile trip from Calgary. We entered the storm front, encountering rain and winds, at the edge of the mountains. As we proceeded, the winds and rain became ever more violent. When we arrived at the Banff Park Gates we were informed that about a foot of snow had fallen earlier that morning. Since then the snow had melted and the precipitation had turned to icy rain which was now falling in torrents. The wind blew at gale force with gusts over eighty miles per hour.

My wife asked why we didn't just go home, since the weather was so bad that we would never be able to take our walk as planned. Normally that is what I would have done and agreed that going further didn't appear to be sensible. But, I explained, the walk had assumed great importance to me. It had become a symbol of my love for her and I still held a conviction that it would be sunny and warm at Johnson's Canyon. I admitted my belief was out of all proportion to reality but not out of proportion to my love. I asked for her agreement to continue. Dubious, she nevertheless consented to go the extra few miles.

The day darkened. We were forced to proceed slowly, the windshield wipers unable to cope with the flood pouring from the ladened sky. Visibility diminished to a few tens of feet. Lashed by deluges of rain and buffeted by the screaming winds, I wondered if we might be blown off the road. No other car passed us. We felt lost and alone in the tempest.

We continued on past the turnoff to the town of Banff as the storm increased its intensity even more violently with every mile. However, I confidently held my vision of the Canyon on a warm, calm, late summer's day. I pictured trees with golden leaves not blown away by violent winds, and red bushes still in leaf. I imagined that I could smell the dried, dusty leaves and grasses unwashed by rains and hear the mountain silences undisturbed by storm.

Abruptly, just a few hundred feet from the Canyon, the wind died. The sun shone. At the entrance to the Canyon, we parked the car and got out. It was a lovely late fall day, as only autumn in the mountains can be.

With joy in my heart and the sun warming our backs, we walked down the dry trail together. We saw the fall colors, accentuated by the brilliance of the day. No winds had swept away the scarlet and golden leaves of those trees and bushes. The creek waters were laughing and the spray of the waterfalls showered diamonds in the sunlight. It was as perfect as I had envisioned. I delighted in the closeness with my wife and with all of nature.

We returned to our car after a leisurely two and a half hours spent walking, climbing and picnicking at the trail's end, my wife remarking on how lucky we had been with the weather. Whereas the Canyon had permitted only small glimpses of the heavens, a full expanse of sky was visible from the parking lot. Looking up, I could hardly believe what I was seeing. We were standing at the base of an enormous cylinder, within a mighty pillar of calm and warmth and light. High above at the top of this cylinder was the blue sun-filled sky. The walls were the purple-black storm clouds.

As these clouds reached the boundary of that cylinder, a fearful force violently repelled them. They were angrily flung upwards and back. They encountered an insurmountable barrier, like the high walls and buttresses around a medieval city, designed to repulse wild barbarians. Within these walls, all was peace and tranquility while the storm raged in frustration and futility outside. The dimensions of this cylinder were such that its diameter was limited precisely to the area where I had envisioned we would walk!

I shivered in awe and wonder. I felt that, while my intense desire for a warm sunny walk up Johnson's Canyon was not exactly the cause, it had triggered terrifying forces far beyond my understanding. A protective web was woven to shield that precise place. Some Greater Power set aside the Laws of Storms.

I've been in Arctic blizzards. I have seen tornados. I have experienced tropical hurricanes. Hurricanes have an eye — a center of calm such as that cylinder. But the eye moves, while this cylinder of sun and light and calmness had remained stationary while the storm, for hours, raged all around the exact spot where I wanted to walk. Never before, or since, have I seen or even heard of anything like it.

I humbly raised my arms to the sky and gave a silent prayer of gratitude for having my need fulfilled and for the honor of witnessing such power. Then, moving my arms, I said aloud, "Thank you! The storm can now do what storms do. All blocks are removed from its progress. It is free to vent its fury as it is meant to do."

Leaving, we drove but a hundred yards and then crossed the edge of the cylinder. Once more we were buffeted by huge torrents of rain. Trees and bushes, stripped of all leaf, bent with the gale. The storm's wild fury outside the pillar was undiminished.

Chapter 7

Funny Things Happened on the Way to Nirvana

I spend the day at the University obtaining information on post-graduate studies. How good it would be to enroll here, living close to Papa once more.

Dinner is ready when I return—he'd poached the salmon I caught yesterday. Afterwards, as I sip a second glass of wine, I state, "That was heavy stuff, that information on prayer. Hope I remember it all. Tonight I'd like to discuss something not so serious, particularly after my day at the University `cause that gave me a lot to think about too."

"Fine. What do you have in mind?"

"How about psychic phenomena? Do you have any theories about it? Like, how does it work and why can't we use it all the time? Are psychics enlightened? And what exactly is psychic in the first place anyway?"

"A good subject and, as you suggest, it's one that shouldn't be taken too seriously. A Hindu fable about a ferry-boat man (in India there are always stories about ferry-boat men) explains why this is so. . . .

The Ferryboat Man

Once upon a time, a hermit who had spent 25 years in a cave — meditating and contemplating and doing all the usual things one does in a cave in India — decided that enough was enough. Dressed in his Sunday-best loincloth and putting on a little straw hat for shade, he left his humble home and made his way to the river, a day or two's journey on foot. At the river there was (you guessed it) a ferryboat man who had just rowed to shore and discharged a passenger.

After requesting that the ferryboat man take him across the river, the Saint — if we wish to call him that —

was informed that there was a fee of two cents (obviously this was before inflation was invented).

"But I don't have any money," explained the poor Saint.

"Then I will not take you across the river," replied the ferryboat man, clearly not wishing to set a nasty precedent for free trips.

The Saint then removed his hat from his head and tossed it into the river. The hat immediately enlarged to become a raft and the Saint jumped into the raft and floated safely to the opposite shore.

"Wow, a miracle!" said the passenger from the ferryboat who had seen and overheard everything. "Is that not the most wonderful thing you have ever seen?"

"Oh?" said the ferryboat man, " So, what's so wonderful? For 25 years he stays in a cave and doesn't learn anything worth two cents!"

While I don't negate psychic experiences, my attitude toward them is akin to that of the ferryboat man. No undue importance should be attached to them. One great lesson they teach us; we are much more than just a material body. Inasmuch as such experiences are independent of time, space and matter, they are non-physical. And if there is a non-physical reality and we are aware of it, then we must also have a non-physical or spiritual component.

Most of us, I am sure, have had experiences that seem out of the ordinary. Examples of telepathy (knowing other people's thoughts) or clairvoyance (knowing about events distant in time or space) have been demonstrated and written about too often for me to bore you with examples. But some other kinds of psychic phenomena are less frequently experienced — like some of the personal experiences I'd like to tell you about.

Telekinesis

In the early 1930's, Dr. J.B. Rhine, a Psychologist at Duke University in Durham, North Carolina, decided to disprove, once and for all, the existence of psychic phenomena. Instead, after developing and conducting several statistically verifiable experiments, he successfully proved, contrary to his expectations, that it actually did exist.

During the early 1940's, when I first discovered Rhine's work, I literally devoured his books. His experiments verified what I already knew from experience: that we all are, at least in part, non- physical, spiritual.

In 1958, I was retained as a consultant to a large chemical company with headquarters in the northeast U.S., not far from Duke University. Availing myself of the opportunity to visit the campus, I travelled there one afternoon and introduced myself to the faculty of the Parapsychology Department, headed by Dr. Rhine. Their hospitality was most warm and I was generously invited to attend their weekly get-together, an informal session where each psychologist reviewed the progress in his or her particular field of investigation. Then they surprised and flattered me by asking me what I had experienced and learned of psychic phenomena. A very lively conversation ensued.

Later, I toured their laboratory with one of the scientists and viewed the machines and games they had developed to identify and measure various psychic phenomena. I was free to examine and use them, as I wished. We continued the conversation of the seminar which was fresh in our minds, especially our discussion about gambling and of people who were consistent winners. As we strolled through the lab, we continued to speculate as to how such people, myself among them, could sometimes influence the roll of the dice or turn of a card.

The movement of matter through space by the power of the mind alone is called telekinesis. One machine for testing this phenomenon consisted of a table six feet long and three feet wide, ruled in large squares, with a raised edge or wall around the rim, like the cushion on a billiard table. At one end was an inclined plane, with five large wooden dice seated at the top in a small holder or cradle. An electric button released a mechanism that allowed the two-inch cubes to roll down the slope and across the table. The purpose of the game was to allow the participant, standing beside the table, to influence the fall of the dice by mind power alone. The squares on the table then allowed the results to be tabulated for statistical analysis.

Without trying to influence the dice, I operated the machine a few times, putting the dice in the cradle and then pressing the button to release them. The dice fell at random over the table. I then announced that I would attempt to influence the dice to come towards me. The dice continued to find random resting places all over the table. After a few more rolls, with no apparent result, I announced that I would next attempt to influence the dice to move away from me.

Suddenly, a sensation of immense power surged through me. I knew I could move the dice. That power could move anything. I then pressed the electric button and released the dice. One of them ended up in the center. Two were tight against the far wall. The fourth had actually jumped the little wall and was on the floor. And the fifth? It had flown 30 feet across the room, hit the wall of the lab with considerable force and landed in the furthest corner.

"Hey! We've never had dice fall off the table before. Do it again!" said the astonished scientist.

I refused. Scientific verification of a particular phenomenon demands innumerable repetitions of the experiment with the same result. Tasting the ocean once is sufficient proof to the non-scientific community that the ocean is salty. And moving the dice once was proof enough to me that it could be done.

Levitation

Not to be confused with "astral travel", where the mind or soul seems to leave the body and go a-travelling by itself, levitation refers to the rising and movement of the physical body itself through the air.

There is a large sect, followers of an Indian swami, who believe that flying or levitation is the hallmark of enlightenment. Students spend tens of thousands of dollars and months, or even years, attempting to achieve this exalted ability. I have yet to hear of anyone's success in flying at will but I'm sure the Guru's bank balance is flying. If you really want to fly, I strongly recommend that you buy airline tickets. It's a whole lot faster — and a whole lot cheaper.

Examples of levitation, however, have been witnessed and recorded through history. St. Francis of Assisi was witnessed to levitate while at prayer, and the Catholic church reports that there was once a flying monk, Saint Joseph of Cupertino. Apparently when one came looking for this particular individual, they never knew which of the eight corners of the room he might be occupying. No less an authority than Pope Urbain the Eighth testified that he himself had witnessed the Saint flying.

I've had one experience in levitation. At the time, I had been in a meditation retreat in Switzerland for over a month. During one particularly lengthy meditation, I felt that something unusual had happened — and on opening my eyes, I found that, while I was still in my chair, both the chair and I were suspended in the air, my hair not quite touching the ceiling. I took a look around the room below — my bed, the extra chair, my clothes scattered where I had left them, the writing table and wardrobe.

Then I started to wonder how I might get down without injury. "Oh, I'll just get down the way I got up," I thought, "slowly and safely", whereupon I closed my eyes again and continued my meditation. An hour later, I opened my eyes and found myself still sitting in my chair but safely on the floor once more.

In astral travel, the body is left behind and may be seen lying where the" soul" has left it. In the circumstance I've just described, I did not see my body below and was aware of my physical self near the ceiling. I had levitated and while it was a very interesting experience, I had no wish ever to repeat it. Again — once was enough. The following story explains why — and why I had no desire to develop or increase any psychic powers.

The Conquering Prince

The Hindus, who seem to have examined everything associated with spirituality, have a story (they always have a story) to illustrate what they feel is the correct attitude towards psychic experiences —

Once upon a time, there was a warrior Prince who wished to invade and conquer the neighboring land. Gathering his large army and resources around him, he crossed the border and occupied the first small village he came to. Then he came to a town. Conquering the town took a little longer. Then he moved deeper into the country and came to a city. He lay siege and, in a month, the city fell to him. Then, spreading through the countryside, he conquered all the surrounding villages, all the towns and all the cities except one.

After years of struggle and conquest, he arrived

ultimately at the capital city where he once more lay siege. By this time, his forces and supplies and energy were sadly depleted by the efforts of his previous conquests, so the capital successfully resisted his weakened efforts. Tired, worn out and defeated, he was forced to retreat to his own country.

Once upon a time, there was another Prince who also wished to conquer a neighboring land. Gathering his large army and resources around him, he crossed the border and, ignoring all the villages and towns and cities along the way, he made directly to the capital and lay siege. His troops were fresh, his supplies sufficient. His will was irresistible. The capital was won, and as a consequence, all the villages, towns and cities which were under the jurisdiction of the capital were also his to rule and to do with as he pleased.

The neighboring land represents the spiritual quest and the capital represents enlightenment or self-realization which, in the Hindu view, should be our ultimate objective. The other cities, towns and villages are all the things that trap and distract us from achieving it, traps such as power, greed, lust and sloth. And psychic phenomena. The closer one is to enlightenment, the more frequently these psychic powers manifest. Because of their wonder and charm, they are the subtlest and most dangerous of all the traps that ensnare and side-track us from enlightenment. Nothing I've just said negates the tender and meaningful impact these experiences usually have when they occur. When they happen, enjoy them, profit by them and accept them as gifts. The great lesson they teach us, however, is that there is a further reality beyond the one we know. And, as in the parable, once that reality is achieved, all else is ours.

The Nature of Psychic Phenomena

Psychic experiences, as I mentioned, are not confined by the laws of time and space and are, by definition, non-physical and therefore connected to a spiritual reality beyond our material world. When psychic happenings such as instantaneous healings, telekinesis and so on, occur, whether we are conscious of it or not, we act as a conduit for the infinite power of that reality— much as a wire conducts electricity. While the power flows through us, seeming miracles can happen.

Other psychic occurrences, such as telepathy and clairvoyance, take place when we have a leak in our "filter". What is meant by that? The spirit-self that we are, knows and is aware of everything. But our finite brain is incapable of absorbing and processing all this knowledge on a continual basis. And even if it could, of what possible value would the knowledge be to us? Of what use is it, for example, for you and me to know that some Bushman in Australia is about to eat a rabbit. . . . or that an Eskimo has been patiently waiting for 5 hours and 37 1/2 minutes to spear a seal . . . or that some woman in Mongolia wants her man to fetch water?

Our brain has an effective filtering system to keep out useless, extraneous information. Only at certain moments, often times of great stress, does that filtering system break down or "leak", permitting the entry of knowledge ordinarily beyond our normal consciousness. At these times, some psychic occurrences — like the visitation of a recently departed loved one or a warning of impending disaster — can be a great blessing.

But those who try consistently to cultivate and expand their psychic powers, are really only cultivating a leak in their filters. And who needs a leaky brain!

Yet when we have a spontaneous psychic experience, we cannot help being fascinated. Let me tell you about other phenomena.

The Cloud

One of the greatest psychic healers I ever met was Feliciano Ormiles who had been a psychic surgeon in the Philippines. He had acquired his knowledge of psychic surgery from his father who had learned it in turn from his father, the skills having been handed down within the Ormiles family for countless generations. Psychic surgeons are able to painlessly penetrate a patient's body with their hands and extract vile-smelling matter which relieves all symptoms of disease and illness. Their ability to perform this type of surgery has been sufficiently studied and verified that today there is little doubt of the authenticity of the phenomenon, called psychic surgery.

I once spent several delightful days in San Diego learning and working with Ormiles whose great joy was in helping others. His charming wife told me the following story about this kind, humorous man when they were living on their farm north of San Jose, in the high mountainous plateau of Costa Rica —

> "In the dry season, the sun shines hot from dawn to dusk in a startling blue sky. Clouds seldom appear, let alone any rain, and naturally the crops wither without water. On our farm all watering was routinely done by hand, the water being procured from a hand-drawn well — an extremely tedious, boring and back-aching job.
>
> "One particular summer, I had told Feliciano for several days that he should be watering the crops. He postponed doing it each day, sometimes with an excuse, sometimes with none.
>
> "Finally, in exasperation — the crops were now in danger of dying — I demanded that he delay no longer and water the wilting plants right away. Then I went about my own chores inside the house. Two hours later I came outside to find Feliciano sitting half asleep in a chair, enjoying the sunshine and the mountain air.
>
> "I was furious, but just before my anger could boil over, it was short-circuited by an unbelievable sight. There was a small cloud in the sky — a solitary cloud. A cloud in the middle of the dry season. As it drifted closer to a position exactly over our fields, its color changed from white to the darker grey of a rain cloud. And then a miraculous refreshing rain began to fall, soaking our thirsty crops with life-giving water.

"A short time later, the rain stopped and the little cloud, now white and bereft of water, slowly drifted away and dissolved into the blue sky.

"I told Feliciano (here she laughed) 'Feliciano, sometimes I think you're the laziest man on earth!'"

Rubber Ice

Today, across the northern Prairies, do children still know about "rubber ice", and do they still venture out on it, risking icy soakings and the fiery wrath of irate mothers?

In early spring on the Prairies, as the run off from the melting snow lies unabsorbed on the still hard-frozen ground, it collects to form ponds in the small dips across the gently rolling landscape. These often become coated with a thin skin of ice as the temperature falls just below freezing overnight, and the ice, less than half an inch thick and heavy with underlying water, gains a certain elasticity. Hence, "rubber ice".

In the Manitoba springtime of my childhood, one of my greatest joys was to search out such a rubber-ice pond and then gathering our gang together, to spend a happy hour or two challenging each other to cross it. The best ponds for the purpose were less than forty feet across but deeper than our knee-high rubber boots — so that when catastrophe finally struck, we were assured of the calamity of wet boots, socks and pant-bottoms.

Having found the "perfect" pond and tested it at the shoreline for its rubberiness, each of the boys in our gang then braved himself for the venture ahead. Little sisters, of course, remained in their safe, appointed places on shore — the challenge of rubber ice being only for us "men". Sisters had a twofold function — to admire our bravery or, when it was their own brother's turn to go, to scream imprecations like "You get off there!" or "You know what Mother told you!" or "Boy, are you going to get it when you get home!"

One particular spring morning I took the courage to be the first to cross the pond. Everybody knew that if anyone was reckless enough to walk in ordinary fashion across rubber ice, it would simply break. A special technique was necessary — a technique so demanding that only the most adept could succeed in making it to the opposite shoreline without tragedy. I had to make myself "light."

First I filled my lungs so completely that they almost burst. If breathing became necessary — as it always did, given the fear and excitement of the moment — only the smallest and shallowest of breaths were taken so as to deplete the minutest amount of air possible. Filled to bursting, I became a balloon — or as light as one, at least.

Next, and just as important, I hunched my shoulders as high as possible, contracting my stomach against my rib cage. This way I figured nearly all my weight was in the top half of my body so that hardly any weight touched the ice.

Now being light, lungs filled, shoulders hunched, arms held away from the body for greater lift and spreading my legs, already stiff with tension, I cautiously shuffled forward. Always keeping both feet on the ice to ensure maximum weight distribution, I shuffled . . . paused . . . then continued to shuffle my way slowly towards the center, as the ice cracked loudly around me, sending fractures like minor earthquakes to the shore — and shivers of fear and excitement up my spine. Encouraged by the gang, showing off for the girls, and mightily urged on by my little sisters' dire warnings, I continued until I reached the opposite side, my pent-up breath expelled in a triumphant cheer.

It was usually safest to be brave and among the first to go. By the time Little Eddie who was the least brave (and the youngest) was forced by mounting peer pressure onto the ice, it had lost much of its elasticity. Repeated bendings into the underlying water had saturated and weakened it, with the result that the center was overlain by water — the slickest, slipperiest surface in the world. Little Eddie never did learn how to walk properly on rubber ice. Hoping to get through the ordeal as fast as possible, he recklessly walked towards the pond's center ignoring our shouted instructions to shuffle slowly and make himself light. Suddenly he froze as a loud ominous 'CRACK' foretold his doom. The ice began to sink. The water welled up around his feet.

In panic he tried to run back. Running was futile. Faster and faster, his feet churned on the collapsing watery ice as he was sucked, slipping and sliding, towards the vortex of the pond's center. Now the waters gushed over the top of the icy surface. A second later the ice broke. The pond's "sacrificial lamb" plunged eight or even ten inches into the abysmal depths of murky ice water amid screams from both victim and audience.

Like the sun rising to a brave new day, the "sacrifice" started up, so filled with adrenaline that he barely felt the shocking chill of the water. He who had been victim was now transformed into hero. Soaked to the skin, slipping on submerged pieces of ice, Little Eddie sloshed and parted the mighty waters before him to rejoin the adulating mob on the shore — the bravest of the brave, infused with courage enough to face even the wrath of Mother!

When I recall these memories, I sometimes wonder if we really did become weightless when we made ourselves "light." We believed we did. Perhaps we really did?

Inside Michelangelo

1968. I was in Rome. For several days I had worked long hours on reviewing geophysical and geological data prior to submitting a request to the Italian government for permits to explore and drill wells for oil and gas in the Adriatic Ocean off the east coast of the country. My research complete, I had decided to ask for three permits. Each had to be accompanied by an enormous amount of detailed information — not simply in duplicate, but in sets of nine copies each!

While draftsmen were preparing the required 27 maps, and typists were typing 27 copies of the Italian translations of my written applications, and financial statements were being duplicated 27 times, and a lawyer was preparing affidavits to be sworn, declarations to be declared, warranties to be warranted and guarantees to be guaranteed, each with 27 copies, I had a free day. No work to do! I could finally be an ordinary tourist and see some of the wonders and glories of this ancient city.

Early in the morning, after a continental breakfast of fresh orange juice, strong aromatic coffee and a roll, I meandered through Rome's parks and winding streets to the Vatican, arriving at the doors of St. Peter's Basilica just as it was opening. Guides conversant in most of the languages of the world were available to escort small groups, or you could simply rent a tape and tape player for the same purpose. I opted to walk alone without help through the structure, following my own intuition and trusting that I would understand most of what I saw.

Taking my time, I absorbed the beauty and atmosphere like a sponge. I was moved to pity as I stared at the Pieta, that statue in alabaster marble of Mary holding the body of her crucified son. I stared too at the crowds of small- statured women in front of the Pieta, all dressed in black — black stockings stuck in black shoes, black skirts, black sweaters covering black blouses — with dark, work-gnarled hands clutching the ends of the black shawls that covered their black hair. I was impressed by the fear on their faces as, repeatedly crossing themselves, they shrank before the lifelike image of their God, dead in the arms of his mother.

After St. Peter's, I strolled through the Vatican Museum. Room after room, treasure after treasure, heap upon heap, pile after pile — pictures, vases, carvings and castrated statues with plaster fig leaves covering their wounds. Hours passed. I went from delight to delight until, like someone who has eaten too much, I could absorb no more. At this moment, I saw a sign with the information that the Sistine Chapel lay ahead. I joined what had become a crowd and, as we proceeded slowly down a narrow passageway, I tried to recall what the Chapel was so famous for. I knew I should know, but couldn't remember.

Then suddenly, the passage opened and I was in the Chapel. Of course! There, at the far end, was the Last Judgement. And there was the ceiling covered with Michelangelo's masterpiece. Imitating a few of the other tourists, I laid down on the floor, the better to gaze and gaze and lose myself.

Thanks to Michelangelo's technique for creating three-dimensional effects, the ceiling above me was filled with exquisite angels and chubby cherubim, their colors so bright and vivid and fresh that the air danced with aliveness. I became so involved and entranced that I seemed to be inside Michelangelo's mind, feeling his feelings, appreciating his sensitivity and knowing exactly what sensations and meanings he wished his paintings to convey. I don't know how long I stayed there, I was lost in time.

One of his tableaux impressed me even more than the others. It was the well-known image of God stretching and straining to touch the hand of Man while Man extended his arm in desultory fashion towards God, his head turned away and his attention given to worldly matters that lay in the opposite direction.

About a year later, I returned once again to Rome

after successfully obtaining two of the three permits for which I had applied from the Italian government. Again, I took the opportunity to visit the Vatican, this time with two companions. Acting as their guide, I took them through St. Peter's and the Museum, and then, with much anticipation, I led them to the Sistine Chapel, the highlight of my previous visit. But this time, much to my amazement, the glorious paintings were time worn and faded, covered with centuries of accumulated dust and grime. What had happened to the bright, vivid colors I had seen before?

Only then did I realize what I had experienced the first time. I had seen the paintings as they had first been painted or even, perhaps, as they had first been visualized by Michelangelo. Our minds had touched across the centuries and I had known exactly what he wished to portray and declare about himself and his God.

Something else had also changed since my first visit. In the tableau that had so impressed me, while God still strained to touch Man, Man was now facing God and also striving to touch the hand of his Creator. That held a deep meaning for me. Intent on building my oil company, I worked 80 to 90 hours a week. All my attention and energies were focused on achieving material success — my attention was not on my spiritual growth. I had since had a most successful and financially rewarding year. My material goals had nearly all been achieved and it was time to take another large step forward to enrich the tapestry of my life. The time was coming, in other words, to lessen my involvement in my business and professional life and to focus my attention on my spiritual journey — just as Man in the tableau had now turned his head toward God.

The Song the Cosmos Sings

A few years ago there was a movie based on Gurdjieff's book "Meetings with Remarkable Men." Gurdjieff was an Armenian philosopher and mystic who, in the early 1900's, taught first in Russia, then in the U.S.

The movie, filmed in Afghanistan, opened with Gurdjieff as a young boy journeying with his father through the valleys of the magnificent and austere desert mountains of that land. After crossing a mountain pass, they descended to a valley and joined a large crowd assembled there. The mood was festive — canvas stalls had been erected and a variety of food was being cooked, sold and eaten. Dust hung heavy in the air and people and animals milled chaotically together, each happily preoccupied with their own concerns.

In the center of the valley was a raised square platform. On one side, seated on their woven rugs, were several stern, bearded Patriarches and on the other, men with various exotic musical instruments. Without any apparent signal, the crowd sensed it was time to begin. Together they drew closer to the platform and complete silence fell.

One of the musicians stepped forward and played a short, eerie tune. Silence ensued. The musician, looking disappointed, returned to his rug. It appeared that some sort of contest was in progress. Another and then a third player performed briefly. Each time the performance was followed by a resounding silence, broken only as the next musician took his place before the crowd. Each, playing his own unique instrument, made his own distinct, eerie sound or melody.

Finally, one more musician stepped forward and began to perform. Advertisements for horror movies like to say that "your hair will stand on end" if you attend their show. Except for one previous occasion, I'd never had that experience myself, and never in a horror movie. Yet as I heard that music, I suddenly had a precognition of what was to come next and the hairs on the back of my head actually did stand up.

He finished playing and again, silence followed.

Then, with a fuller, louder sound, the mountains reverberated. Non-human sources sang within those ancient rocks and the whole strange song came flowing back in ever greater crescendos. When the music ended, the vibrating resonance slowly stilled. Then the Patriarches nodded and the smiling contestant was awarded a lamb as his prize.

The crowd began to disperse. They had heard their miracle. Gurdjieff was told that the people gathered in this spot every other decade in hopes of hearing the mountains sing. They would gather again in another twenty years.

When the hairs on my neck "stood on end", I was reminded of the experience I had had the previous year —

I was vacationing with a dear friend at Poipu Beach on the Hawaiian Island of Kauai. My rented apartment was right on the beach where the sound of the surf sang me to sleep each night. One late afternoon, after shutting the doors and windows for optimum quiet, we sat side by side meditating. After an hour's deep meditation we opened our eyes and smiled at each other. Then, our eyes again closed, we quietly began to chant the universal mantra, "Aum" together. After a few minutes we stopped chanting and enjoyed the silence within ourselves as the surf softly and rhythmically pounded outside.

Then the chanting started again, softly at first, then louder and louder. I opened my eyes and glanced quickly at my companion, but her lips weren't moving, nor was she making any sound. The air vibrated, the floor, ceiling, walls, beach, ocean — everything resonated, "Aum, Aum, Aum." Our quiet chanting was flowing back to us in ever louder crescendos and the hairs on my head stood on end — not from fear, but in awe and electrified by the vibration of 'Aum'.

When the chanting finally ceased, I sat quietly in the silence, broken only by the muffled sighing of the surf.

When I opened my eyes, I looked wonderingly at my companion and asked her, "Did you hear what I heard?"

"The chanting? I thought maybe you were doing it at first," she replied, "so I opened my eyes. When I discovered that you were silent, I closed them again and just listened. Never heard anything like that before. I think we've heard the hum of the Universe, the song the Cosmos sings."

Chapter 8

Lessons Along the Way

How much do I believe of what Papa told me last night, I wonder? Like levitation. Did that really happen? Not that I would ever think that the old man lied. But maybe he'd been dreaming?

Finishing breakfast but not waiting to clear the table, I begin, "I'd like to get back to more practical matters. All that psychic stuff was interesting but there are a lot of other things I want to talk about. I need to know how to cope with life, to handle my day to day problems. How does a person go about learning those things?"

As usual, he takes a moment before he answers . . .

Knowledge is gained and life's problems solved in such varied ways - logical reasoning, past experiences, intuition, insights, revelations, books, stories, fables, parables, the example of others and so on. Always we must be awake, expectant, for sometimes answers come in a curious fashion. For example, one time I was in a quandary over whether to invest in a small business venture that two industrious young women wished to start. One day while walking along a busy street and mentally analyzing the pros and cons, I casually passed a man who was carrying two large bags of groceries.

"Leave the girls alone," he warned emphatically .

I could scarcely believe what I'd heard. I ran after him to demand some explanation. To my astonishment I discovered that he was mentally disturbed and was merely babbling random phrases. I considered, however, I had received the answer that I needed and did not invest, which later events proved to be a very fortunate decision.

Life constantly presents situations and circumstances which are the lessons we need to learn in order to grow. If we don't learn the first time, we encounter the same problem again and again. Each time the problem seems bigger, more difficult, like a wall that grows higher and higher and is increasingly difficult to scale. For instance, I used to have a fear of speaking in public. When I went into business for myself, it was imperative to speak in public in order to sell my services. Having repeatedly avoided it until then, my wall had grown very high. It took considerable effort to tear it down.

I have never met anyone from whom I could not learn something. I honor each of my many, many teachers — my parents, friends, educators, sages and those who have left a legacy of learning in books. Yet experience itself is our best teacher as this ancient Chinese parable asserts;

Tell me - I forget;
Show me - I may remember;
But let me experience it and then I'll know it!

And so it is that experiences have taught me most of life's lessons and crystallized my philosophy. I'll share some of them with you but first I'd like to commence with an allegory which has held deep meaning for me.

Chan Chi'en

For millennia, China had a great, enlightened and progressive civilization whose stability rested on a highly educated civil service. Youths that mustered good marks in primary school were given more education and, commensurate with the degrees of learning they obtained, were rewarded with administrative positions within the government. Demonstration of skills at one level of administration led to ever greater opportunities for advancement. During this time, over one thousand years ago, a brilliant man, Chan Chi'en, had risen to be Governor of one of the Provinces. Chan Chi'en did not glory in the title and honor he had received but, rather, regarded it as his duty to serve his nation and fulfill the trust placed in him, to the best of his ability.

Chan Chi'en's inclination was to a quiet, contemplative life and not a political or authoritative position. While he enjoyed philosophical discussions with close friends, he found his greatest joy in nature's solitude. He had a small hut built in the wilderness beside a mountain lake and, whenever his duties permitted, he would go there, travelling up a stony path on a little donkey. When it was time to leave, he returned reluctantly, for his heart remained at his sanctuary. It became his custom on the returning journey to sit backwards on his donkey so he could contemplate his beloved lake and mountains and forest as long as possible.

One day, while the donkey slowly picked its way over the loose rocks on the downward trail, it occurred to Chan Chi'en that this was the proper way to go through life: looking backward, being introspective. The sights along the trail glided past him; a rocky outcrop, a tall pine tree, a stream, a waterfall, a squirrel, a flower, a brightly colored bush. He observed and appreciated, reacting to each sight and event as it passed. So, he thought, when events in life come to pass, their value lies, not in their occurrence, but rather in one's reaction to them. Many are the incidents in life: an unkind word, a sincere thank you, a joke shared, a promotion, being fired, falling in love, the breaking of a relationship, a triumph, a failure, a birth, a death. These events happen and pass into our memory. By looking backward, one can examine whether one's reaction to them was good and thereby learn to improve one's behavior in the times ahead.

"Certainly", Chan Chi'en thought, " I set my goal and choose my path even as I set the donkey on the homeward trail but, when things happen in my life, I am responsible for how I react. I am not necessarily responsible for what happens but I am entirely responsible for myself. I, alone, am responsible for what I think, what I feel, what I say, what I do".

And now, to tell you what and how I've learnt from some of the events in my life.

The Blessing of Pain

How far blood spurts when the wrist is slashed!

In 1942, during the summer break from university, I obtained a job at the Eldorado Radium Refinery in Port Hope, Ontario. Here four products were produced: radium for cancer therapy; a radium salt for painting items such as the hands on watches so that they glowed in the dark; uranium nitrate for use as a yellow pigment in ceramics; and the black powder, uranium oxide.

The refinery, surrounded by a ten foot heavy chain-link fence, had the highest priority rating in war-time Canada. Uranium oxide which had previously been a product with little demand was now, for some unknown reason, in very heavy demand and was shipped in ever-increasing quantities to a "Manhattan Project". In the lab we used to wonder what use was being made of the black powder. When I suggested perhaps some sort of bomb was being made, the Chief Chemist told me not to be stupid and that even if such a thing as an atomic bomb was possible, it would take decades of work to accomplish it. Three years later, when my conjecture was proven true, I thought how curious it was that the greatest pain I experienced in life was connected to the weapon that caused the greatest pain in so many other lives.

In the refinery I was employed in the production of uranium nitrate, the yellow pigment used in pottery, which was made by a fractional crystallization process. Ceramic saucer-shaped vessels or vats about four feet in diameter held a hot soup of uranium and concentrated sulphuric and nitric acids. Beautiful crystals of brightest yellow slowly crystallized out of that deadly broth. Part of my job, working with one other university student employed for the summer, was to ladle the remaining liquid from these vats, after the crystals had formed, into ceramic carboys or large jars about 2 1/2 feet high. When full they weighed in excess of 120 pounds. Our task then was to pour the hot liquid contents into alternative vats which were in the earlier stages of crystallization.

One particular night, we were alone in the refinery except for the night watchman as the rest of the plant was temporarily shut down while expanding the facilities. It was about nine o'clock and we had just filled a carboy with the heavy liquid. Each lifting it by a handle, we lugged it to an appropriate vat. Then raising it high, I placed my right hand underneath, in preparation for pouring.

With no warning, the carboy shattered, and a jagged piece severed my right wrist. For a split instant I saw the white bone inside my arm and then, as the momentarily blocked blood burst from the cut artery, a red stream shot at an angle to the ceiling, perhaps fifteen or twenty feet away!

"Let's get to the First Aid," I shouted. We ran upstairs while I held my arm to minimize the bleeding as best I could.

The First Aid cabinet, made of metal, had a large padlock on it. It was locked to prevent pilfering!

"I've got to get out of here, get to the hospital", I yelled.

Running down the stairs, through the dark refinery, out the door, across the yard to the gate, we discovered it too was locked for security reasons. "You go one way. I'll go the other. Find the watchman!"

A moment or two later, I heard a shout; the watchman had been found. I hurried back to the now opened gate and ran to the street outside. Then I hitch-hiked! A car stopped. We drove to town. We stopped for an instant while someone jumped out of the car to phone the hospital to expect us while we sped onwards. I held my arm evermore weakly as my blood continued to spurt and drain .

Upon arrival at the hospital, I got out and walked to the nurse waiting with a wheelchair who then pushed me through the entrance way and into an elevator. Only then did I faint from lack of blood.

The doctor on call that night was an elderly man who had retired several years previously but who, due to the doctor shortage resulting from the war, had returned to work again. As I had lost nearly all my blood, two days passed before I was really conscious. He had successfully sutured the severed tendons and artery, but he either had never learned or had forgotten what nerves were. He was bewildered because I could not move some of my fingers. Later, while probing with his fingers near the wound, he often pressed on the raw, severed end of the nerve. Each time I'd scream and faint. His only comment was, "My, for a big man, you're sure an awful sissy."

After recovering my strength and being discharged from the hospital, I consulted another doctor who confirmed my guess that the ulna nerve had been severed. An operation to repair it was not successful.

I learned much from my experience:

- I learned safety consciousness and, as a result, not one of the hundreds who later worked in my employ was ever seriously injured. Definitely I never locked a First Aid cabinet to prevent pilfering!

- I considered for a short time that with a hand half paralyzed, I had a fine excuse for not doing much with my life. I soon rejected that thought however, and decided I would not be handicapped. Sure, my right hand is partially paralyzed but I am not prevented from doing anything I wish. I seldom even think of it now.

- After the accident, I experienced excruciating pain for many weeks. One day I asked myself, "What is the purpose of pain?" I concluded that a pain was a distress signal sent to the brain by that part of the body that was injured, or under attack by germs or virus or otherwise in need of help. I had received the message from my injured hand and I had done what I could to relieve it. I verbalized this to my arm, thanking it for notifying me and affirming I'd received the message okay, but that I did not need to have the same message repeated time after time. Subsequently, the pain diminished and finally disappeared entirely. Many times I have used this technique to relieve pain. For instance, when a toothache occurs I tell the tooth, "I've received the message. It will be attended to as soon as possible. I do not need to receive the message again." Invariably the aching diminishes or even disappears.

- One night, while still suffering continuous pain, I distinctly heard a voice inside my head say, "Do not ask your pain to go until it has blessed you." I puzzled over that for several days. I had always had a deep-rooted fear, not of being injured but of feeling the hurt, the pain itself. Now I was experiencing the limits of pain. Pain, I discovered, can be tolerated to a certain limit; and up to that limit, there is nothing to greatly fear. Beyond that threshold of pain, the mind simply blanks out, overloads and becomes unconscious, refusing to accept any more 'phone calls' from the body. Once you're unconscious, there is no pain. I was indeed blessed, for my intense fear was eliminated.

The Cosmic Joke

"I appreciate what you're telling me Papa, but my biggest problem is how I feel, how I feel inside. I've got too many problems that I don't know what to do about. It's just too much sometimes."

"What helps me is to remember an ancient Zen

saying: 'There is only one problem: to keep from laughing.'"

"What do you mean? I sure don't feel like laughing about my problems.

Although I enjoy telling a good joke, the Cosmic Joke can only be experienced. As that experience only occurs on a higher plane of reality, the excuse of the poor storyteller, "You would have laughed if you'd been there," is very appropriate. Nevertheless, I shall attempt to tell the joke.

First, it *is* a joke, an hilarious experience. While experiencing the joke, I've laughed until tears have streamed down my face and I've had to hold my stomach from the pain of my laughter. Even then, I might only collapse, rolling on the ground with my knees tight pressed against my chest like a baby and laugh some more.

To see the joke, pretend you are looking down onto the world from a great height. Observe humanity scurrying busily in all directions like a large hill of ants. Observe closer: each individual self-important with his or her separate task, all thinking they have great problems and hurts and fears, each feeling hate, envy, jealousy and depression. See them struggle and squirm but do not sneer for we are seeing ourselves.

The great Joke is this: we're not what we think we are! In reality we are Spirit, untouched by our problems, feelings or actions. Tawdry schemes and futile goals bury our magnificence. We fool ourselves. Frustrated, believing we are weak and helpless, sick and weary, we ignore our power. As if we were insignificant specks in an uncaring world, we forget our Glory. Envious and jealous we fail to accept the Universe for our inheritance. Fearing injury and death we are oblivious to our Immortality.

How seriously we take ourselves. How importantly

we strut. How loudly we complain. Like puppets pulling their own strings, how we dance. Such things we do. How funny. How hilarious.

Laugh! for God is at play. See the cosmic joke—God's joke on Himself.

"Now, Robert, let me tell you about a few other things I've learnt and how they have helped me."

White Light

New York city simmered in a heat wave when I was there in 1965 on business. Onc evening I visited my friend Bert with whom I'd worked in South America and who was one of the most considerate men I ever knew. As we sat on his outdoor patio he asked me what I had done and seen while in town.

I told him the previous evening that Sal, whom we both knew, had invited me to her parents' home in the Bronx. Taking the subway, I arrived at their small apartment wilted from the heat, my fresh shirt wet with perspiration. As well as Sal's parents, several uncles and aunts had gathered to meet me. After the words of welcome and questions about myself, their conversation centered on their problems and greatest fear. Gangs of youths, they informed me, ruled the neighborhood. The police were impotent and any attempt to obtain police help resulted in swift and brutal reprisal. They said that at any moment, their door could be kicked in, and they could be beaten, robbed, raped or killed. To my question of what they might do, they answered that their only solution was to move away from the home they had lived in for 24 years.

Bert added his comments that these Puerto Rican gangs were uncontrollable and recited a grisly episode which I really didn't need to hear. I continued with my description of the previous evening, mentioning the incredible heat in the stuffy apartment where a large hot meal had been prepared. After dinner, Sal suggested that we go for a walk. To Bert's question, I replied that I didn't know exactly where we'd gone, but named two parks we had walked through.

"You walked through those parks? At night? And unarmed, and with a girl? You're not here: you're dead! No one walks through those places," Bert exclaimed in shock. "Good Lord! They are the parks I just told you about. Please don't do that again. I hope your other evenings were tamer."

With slight embarrassment, particularly after his kind solicitation for my welfare, I confessed, "Well, the night before that, I got lost. It was too hot and muggy to stay in my hotel room so I went to the subway and took the first train that came along. The train, too, was stifling, so after half an hour or so, I got off. I didn't know where I was, it wasn't important; I just wanted to walk for awhile and cool off and assumed I could find a return subway when I wished. So walk I did for at least two hours . . . right into Harlem!"

Even our newspapers 2,500 miles away in Western Canada reported the unrest and violence that prevailed in that district at that time. A solitary white person like me was an easy, inviting target.

Bert looked slightly sick, "Whatever did you do? My lord, you really are dead! No one could get out of that."

Briefly I said that I had walked rather quickly for many blocks until I'd found a taxi to return me to my hotel. I did other things as well.

Recognizing my predicament, I walked openly down the middle of the street which was void of traffic. I hoped being in full view gave me some protection as I believed that most citizens of Harlem did not approve of violence and that gangs would hang out in the alleys and side streets. I imagined I had an appointment, that I was expected, that I was already late and walked as fast as I could, my face turned resolutely forward. My eyes however went from side to side and from sight to sight: smog-blackened tenement houses; black bodies draped from every open window in vain hopes of a breath of cooler air; black half-naked bodies crowded onto every step and stoop, wet with perspiration. The only sound was the blare of radio and T.V. It was too hot to talk.

"Why in hell do they stay here and live like this?" I wondered as I thought of the cool forests and mountains and the cold rivers of my homeland. I felt sorry for anyone who lived in such conditions and felt the common bond of our humanity even as I kept strictly to my own business.

I also did something else. I imagined that I was surrounded by a bright light; a white light that guarded and protected me and within which I was safe from harm.

This powerful technique of surrounding oneself with white light can be used anytime one is in danger. I believe that the light really exists, that it surrounds us and fills us. It is the light that created us and sustains us, protects and heals us. It is the eternal Light into which we grow. It is the life force itself, the all-powerful Great Spirit. Consciously surrounding ourselves with it, we are safe from harm. That night I walked in light until I found the taxi that returned me safely to my hotel.

One other curious thing happened during that same New York visit, just prior to my departure. Other than visiting my few friends, I had not enjoyed my trip. The hot smog irritated my skin and a shower gave me only temporary relief. The city was also suffering a serious water shortage at the time and water with a meal was served reluctantly and only on request. Everyone, suffering from the incessant heat, was irritable and easily angered. My meetings had proved unsuccessful and I was disappointed, discouraged and weary as I made my reservations to leave the next morning. After a solitary meal, packing, and a final walk in the lung-scorching smog, I lay on my bed, naked, waiting for sleep to provide release from the heat.

The sweat-soaked sleepless hours passed. In the very early hours, we tend to become philosophical. Laying there, I decided I would never spend time in New York City again. In the future I would work, dwell and visit only beautiful places. It then occurred to me that, if I were never to return, it would be good to pray for the good fortune of New York before I left. The blessing most desperately needed was rain to break the three months of drought and the record heat wave.

First, I visualized the whole State of New York being bathed in a pure white light. Then I prayed, "May all who dwell here be blessed with rain — refreshing, cooling, thirst-quenching rain."

I awoke in the morning to a bed dampened by the night's perspiration. I quickly showered, dressed, paid my bill and then had a hasty breakfast. Grabbing a taxi I headed for the airport, an hour's journey away through angry traffic. As we neared the terminal building, giant muddy drops splashed onto the wind shield. "Hey, look at that. Rain! First in damn near thirteen weeks," said the taxi driver. "Boy, hope it continues and cools things down. We sure do need it."

The rain did continue. Forest fires in Upper New York State were extinguished, the water reservoirs filled, the city streets were washed, and the air was cooled and cleansed. The long drought and heat spell ended.

White light can help and be used in various circumstances. For example, in Canada, years later, I was walking alone along a heavily wooded path at dusk when two men rushed towards me from the bushes on either side. Quickly surrounding myself with white light, I felt its power, and knew they could not penetrate my shield. Knowing I was safe, I calmly continued to walk. They slowed their rush and fell in behind me. They could not touch me. Their footsteps slowed, fell further behind, and finally stopped.

White light can also be used when no danger threatens, but simply when one wishes his way to be cleared of obstacles and obstructions. A case in point: in Hong Kong, where I spent a couple of days after a vacation in Thailand, it was rush hour and I was in an underground subway station for the return trip to my hotel. After being buffeted by the enormous throng of workers anxious to be home from work as soon as possible, I surrounded myself with light. Not one person touched me again. The aura was impenetrable and I was able to walk freely through those hordes as they parted before me.

Realities

While on winter vacations at tropical resorts, it is my habit to arise at first light. Wearing only swimming trunks, I enjoy walking the empty beaches devoid of the hordes of tourists who appear later in the day. I enjoy the cool air on my skin, listen to the birds singing the world awake, see fish jumping on the ocean surface and watch the brightening colors of the clouds as the sun prepares for its grand entrance. Then, returning with the arisen sun, I leisurely swim the last mile back to my hotel.

Early one particular morning, I had walked about two miles along the beach away from the luxurious hotel where I was staying in southwest Mexico, when I observed that another human shared the dawn. Angling my path towards him I discovered an old Zapotec Indian leaning against an overturned fishing boat, mending his nets.

Bidding him a 'Buenas Dias' and receiving a courteous reply, I stopped to talk. Trying to show my intelligence I asked if a shark had caused the damage to his nets.

"Of course", he replied and stared at me in silence as if wondering why a seemingly intelligent man would ask what even a three year old in his village would have known. Replying to his query I informed him I was on vacation from Canada. He pondered the significance of this for a moment or two, then said, "Good". The word was a pronouncement as if the fact I was from Canada explained an awful lot.

"How's the fishing?" I asked, knowing the reply would be one of the two tragedies invariably recited by fishermen the world over. Either the fishing is tragically bad, or the fishing is fair and the prices are tragically bad. His reply was expected, the tragedy at the moment being the price.

His Spanish vocabulary was very limited and thick with the accent of his native Indian dialect, and my Spanish was rusty and partly forgotten, my not having spoken it since I resided in South America ten years previously. Our attempts at conversation became interspersed by ever longer silences. Something seemed to be happening. Somehow we were communicating, we were establishing a rapport, or more exactly, it was as if we were in harmony or communion at some deep silent level within each other. There was a solemn comfort to his presence. I felt honored to be with him.

During these ever-lengthening silences, he stared at the horizon across the ocean. While thus occupied, I studied the dignity of the man — he was barefoot and dressed in tattered trousers, whose jagged threads ended half-way below his knees, and a startling-clean, white shirt which sharply contrasted with the old mahogany color of his skin. Old—how old I could not guess, yet his jet-black hair glistened with health and vigor. His face, dominated by the proud prow of the typical Indian nose, was etched by time, sun and storm. His black liquid eyes, reflecting an inner peace, were in contrast to the lean hardness of his body. His strong sinewy hands were sure and swift at the mending. They were well trained and needed no direction. His feet, exhibiting several scars, looked as if they too were well trained and I pictured them holding or pulling on ropes and fishing lines. Standing in front of this man I felt slightly embarrassed in my white swimming trunks, my pinky-white flesh exposed and a brightly colored hat that screamed 'tourist' hiding my white balding head from the sun.

What was he seeing as he watched the sea? He read it as I read a newspaper. The sea and sky were a vast pageantry rich with the meaning of past and future. It seemed as if he lived in a reality beyond my ken or imagination. He knew a profound yet simple world where sea and sky and life and death were one. He did not think but comprehended everything.

He stared with infinite patience as eternity unfolded before him. He accepted the broken shells on the beach, the newly-built, garish luxury hotels, the rotting fish just above the tide, the pelicans slowly beating their wings a millimeter above the waves, the plastic cup sadly moving back and forth, grinding on the sand with each wave. All was one and properly placed—there was no need to see part as right and part as wrong. No need to close the eyes to this or that. He knew better than to try. The thin path of cloud marking a jet's trail across the sky would soon dissolve, even as all Man's endeavors. The loud tourists laughing and complaining and the tinny tunes from their bars would fade in time. The fancy cabin cruisers would sail away. It was just a temporary madness. He looked beyond with eyes of love and passion to his mistress, the sea. His life was rich with what wonders and marvels I could only guess.

I do not remember what I was idly talking about at

the time but I had made some mention of the World War which was still fresh in everyone's mind. He interrupted me to ask with sharp surprise, "There was a war?"

"Oh yes, the Great World War," I explained.

Silence ensued while he digested this news. Then, "Who fought?", he inquired.

"Oh, Germany and Japan against Britain, America and Russia. Nearly every nation in the whole world was involved."

He stared at the sea, his hands automatically mending his net. After accepting the news as part of the eternal, he asked, "Was my country involved?"

"Oh yes, your country fought bravely!"

After another meaningful silence, thinking of those who must have suffered and died, he wondered aloud, "On whose side?"

"On the side of the Americans," I assured him.

His head nodded once more, accepting all. Time passed. The sun was now above the horizon, the early morning clouds dissolving into the growing warmth of the day. Tourist sounds, the buzz of motor boats, the first calls and yells of guides and hawkers, sounded remote and far away. Turning finally from his contemplation, he asked, "And who won?"

The reality of the Great World War which I assumed had affected everyone in the world in some way had no existence or place in his reality. Although fellow passengers on the same planet hurtling through space, our realities were completely separate and distinct.

On parting, we each bowed slightly to the other — a mere handshake would not have seemed appropriate even if his fingers had not been occupied continuously with the nets. Later, pondering on our meeting, I concluded that each one of us lives in a separate unique reality, bounded not only by what we observe and do, but by our own walled-in beliefs, opinions, cultures and superstitions. In the remote Canadian wilderness I have encountered hermits, trappers and prospectors. The world of these solitary men is also far distant from mine. Similarly each society and race lives in their own universe. Compare, for instance, the extremely different world-views of the Eskimos, the South-Sea Islanders, the desert nomads of Arabia, the citizens of the Bronx, a jungle tribe, and the traditional Japanese.

This realization that we each live within our own reality was reinforced just a week after my meeting with the Zapotec Indian as I strolled through the nearby village with fellow tourists, a couple from northern California.

"Isn't that just awful! I feel sick at my stomach", said my male companion.

Responding to my surprise he explained, "Didn't you see him? That beggar on the corner? It just makes me disgusted to see such poverty and know people have to live like that in Mexico!"

"Oh, I saw him alright," I smiled, "but after living in South America for two and a half years, the thought I had was, "Wow! What a rich country Mexico is. Even its beggars have shoes."

How differently we perceive reality! Two men with whom I had worked many years before, were both laid off when they were 48 years old. One went home, crawled into bed feeling everything was futile and his life finished. Five years later he died painfully, rotted by alcohol and despair.

The other man, similar in experience and education, decided he had been provided with the opportunity to fulfill his dream of being self-employed. Five years later he was financially independent, and enjoying life more than ever. These two men, outwardly equal, were in an identical situation. But each lived within their separate realities. To one it was the end, to the other the start of a new beginning.

Lucky, with whom I worked for several years in both South America and Canada, is another example. He exhibited great confidence and enthusiasm and the oil company which employed him followed his decisive recommendations for drilling wells for several years. Unfortunately and invariably, each well was a bitter disappointment and a very costly failure. He never fulfilled the promise of his nick-name. The company finally gave him a job where he was merely a clerk, a filer of technical data. He was on a shelf, out of harm's way. On his 50th birthday he was forced into early retirement, a polite word for being fired.

Despondent, aware of his failures, he sank into depression. His body deteriorated and he had a series of operations. I thought he would die soon.

The next time I saw him, however, the old Lucky had returned. His step was quick, his eyes shone with excitement, his voice vibrated with energy, and the elegant suit he was wearing proclaimed a new-found wealth.

"After my last operation, something happened," Lucky told me. "I started to look at things differently. The world seemed to change. Reality somehow shifted. Although I'd made mistake after mistake throughout my career, they were different mistakes each time. My misfortune was to always find new mistakes to make. It then occurred to me that others could profit from my errors. So I devised a workshop wherein I disclosed and discussed my mis-interpretations of technical data, my erroneous assumptions, and all my other slips, oversights, flawed reasonings, and overly optimistic hopes. The workshop was a huge success. Soon I was working three months out of the year and earning more than double what my former yearly salary had been. I toured the world teaching wherever there was petroleum exploration—the Middle East, Australia, Great Britain, Europe, Canada, USA. I even went to China once. My health and energy have been restored and together with my wife, we really began to enjoy the other nine months of the year as well—golf and my many hobbies. The lessons learned from all my failures ultimately have become my success in life."

Perhaps mystics are correct who claim everything is Maya, that all is a great illusion. Like Lucky, our lives change as our illusion shifts and we broaden our understanding and perceptions. If together we all changed our illusions, would we not change the whole world? And perhaps, just perhaps, it is our ideas, thoughts and dreams that created the Cosmos in the first place?

Good-bye, Hello, Good-bye

I excuse myself to make a phone call to arrange a meeting with a friend—not one of the party-goers. Something triggers a hollow feeling after I hang up. I feel depressed, sad. I'm alone, so lonely, ever since she left me. Papa sits silently, aware that something's wrong, waiting for me to speak, if and when I wish.

Finally I explain, "Guess I never really told you about my girlfriend. Christine is her name. I suppose what happened is not that unusual but it broke my heart. We met at university and fell deeply in love. I wanted to be with her forever but her career and her parents' demands took precedence. We parted after graduation. Everything seemed to end for me. I still wonder if life is worthwhile without her. Would you like to hear a poem I wrote for her?" I barely contain my emotions.

My Incarnate Love

Your voice is soft yet strange to me,
I do not recognize your face;
Yet you were very dear to me
In another time and place.

Did we build pyramids
To challenge time along the Nile?
Or in the gardens of old Babylon
Did we linger for awhile?

To immortalize your beauty
Did I create the Taj Mahal?
How looked you then? How felt your hands?
Did I plumb your depths, your soul, your all?

Or were we simple peasant folk
Who toiled our weary toil
Yet dreamed our dreams and loved our love
And together tilled the soil?

Perhaps we lived in ancient Mayan time?
Perhaps we fished exotic coral seas?
Or was I St. Francis and you my Clare
In solitude, upon our knees?

Did I imagine it or not:
Sharing our love beside a stream -
Our special secret emerald place?
Or were these fragments of a broken dream?

What other moons dwelt in our sky?
What vivid waters lapped our shore?
What airs were breathed? What shape our frame?
What colored suns did we adore?

Oh I would tear that Maya veil apart!
Against my memory's quicksand I strain
To find incarnate my eternal better part
And closely hold you to my breast again.

I do not see through Death's thick wall
I do not know our other wheres or when.
I only know I love you, here and now,
As deeply as I loved you then.

After the mood of the poem had partly dissolved, Papa said, "Perhaps my experience will help a little . . .

How often do we say hello and good-bye?—I'm not referring to our casual salutations as we pass friends on the street, but to all those important hellos and good-byes as we journey down the street called Life. It's a hello each time we make a new beginning, encounter a new experience, start a new friendship, or instigate a change. With each, we experience the excitement and fear of the unknown for we are suddenly alone, all by ourselves, having said good-bye to old comfortable surroundings and companions. These hellos and good-byes are the steps we take along our life's journey, our own unique, individual and solitary path.

Our casual encounters in daily life are not much different. We greet a friend, obtain the "news", learn all we can. But we don't dally. When we have learned what we can, it's time to say good-bye and continue happily towards our destination.

Parenting teaches us how to say good-bye. Newborn children need constant care and attention, but as they grow, our involvement in their lives decreases. We no longer have to feed or dress them and we cheerfully say good-bye to those tasks. As children continue to mature, the good parent slowly but continuously lets go of control until they stand alone, confident and sure of their place and direction. Yet we never say good-bye to love. The love I had for my children I still have in fullest measure even though not one of them does what I think they should do. And for this too, I give reverent thanks. They express themselves and follow their own destiny.

While for each good-bye in my life there has been at least one new hello, there still seems to have been an awful lot of good-byes, with their accompanying sense of loss and loneliness. Like you, I too lost a great love, a painful good-bye. My most painful good-bye however, was the separation from my wife. We'd accomplished so much together—home, family, career, but new hellos were calling me and different hellos were calling her. Gently we said good-bye.

Hellos to new experiences usually occur after a good-bye. Sometimes more than one good-bye is necessary: for instance, the good-bye of parting from a tender love and then a second good-bye, this time to the grief, the sadness caused by that parting. Somehow there is only room for the new after the old moves out. When I hold on to easy, familiar patterns in my career, relationships and beliefs, I stagnate. When I risk the unknown, life vibrates. When I dare, such marvels are uncovered. As a poet might say, "To reach the Blessed Isles, one must leave the shore."

There is a difference between the aloneness we experience when moving forward on life's path and the experience of loneliness. Loneliness is a feeling resulting from some real or imagined rejection or non-acceptance. In a crowded city we are not alone, yet it can be the loneliest place in the world. By contrast, when we're alone in wilderness we seldom feel loneliness for we experience an acceptance, a togetherness, a unity with the rest of nature.

Never are we really alone. Whereever we go, God is. Our togetherness is inherent even in the word 'good-bye' itself, as it is a contraction of "God Bide" meaning "may God abide with you while we are parted from one another." Similarly, the Spanish "adios", and the French "adieu", both meaning "to God", express the thought, "I give you into God's keeping while we are parted."

And when we say our last good-bye, will we not hear a more profound hello? Good-bye, hello. Good-bye, hello.

"That helps, Papa. But I'm not ready yet to say good-bye to Christine. I can't. It's too soon. The wound's too recent, too raw. I'll try to do it sometime, but not now. I miss her too much."

"Right. Taking time to mourn your loss is a necessary part of the healing process. But put a time limit on it. Decide what day you're going to say good-bye and then move on. Don't get stuck in a morass of regret and feeling sorry for yourself."

"Okay, Papa, I won't. Now, please go on and tell me about other things you've found out."

The Unexpected

Another lesson I learned was to trust my subconscious. Often it has been more reliable than rational reason. At one time or another we've all acted spontaneously and afterwards said 'I did it without thinking' or 'I acted before I could think'. What we did may, in hindsight, seem surprising or even irrational but it worked and was probably the best course of action. It may save your life. It did mine.

A Sunday in March, 1949. One of the two annual "winter" or rainy seasons of the tropics was ending. Our friends in Bogota, Colombia, George and Joan, had invited us to join them on a day's outing into the countryside. This area, lying 9,000 to 11,000 feet above sea level and only a few degrees from the equator, enjoys perpetual springtime. A peaceful pastoral land of low hills, its fields of grass and grains are broken by small rivers and streams and punctuated with the exclamation marks of the tall eucalyptus trees — a land as green as emerald and a sky the color of an aquamarine, like the magnificent jewels mined in this part of the world.

After a picnic lunch George suggested that we drive to a small, nearby town to see if there was anything of interest to explore. We headed along the mud roads of the area, then over the cobblestones of the village's streets to the "socolo" — the town square, typical of Spanish pueblos. Strangely, as we remarked at the time, we didn't see one person along the few blocks to the square, although siesta time had passed. The square, too, was empty and we surmised that some large fiesta or perhaps a bullfight was in progress.

My wife, George and Joan decided to explore along one of the streets off the square where they saw a line of small shops. I had caught sight of the gold and marble steeples of a cathedral glistening in the sun a block or two down another avenue and decided to see if there was a photo worth taking.

Under a startling blue sky, the houses with windowless walls and barred doors formed an empty, stark, white-washed canyon as I went down the street. My footsteps echoed in the silence. Suddenly there was a shout. Uniformed men burst out of a doorway beside me and surrounded me with bayonets. There were twelve of them, their uniforms faded and indistinguishable except for one man with three stripes on his sleeves. That one jabbed his bayonet against my navel. A thirteenth man, slightly better uniformed — their officer — ran behind me and pressed his pistol roughly into the small of my back. I raised my arms as bayonet and pistol continued to jab.

Something had to be done quickly or I'd never do anything again. In Colombia, life was the cheapest commodity and murder and killings commonplace. I acted instinctively, not pausing to think (if I'd thought about it I would never have done what I did!). Slowly lowering my arms, I simulated extreme anger and began to swear. My Spanish vocabulary of obscene words was extensive and using some of the worst, I cursed the soldiers roundly, assuring them that they were completely despicable and attributing to their mothers a most lurid past. Normally this would have roused them to retaliate. Many had been killed in that country for lesser insults. But I had done the unexpected. Daring to curse *them* while *they* held bayonets and guns paralyzed them with surprise.

I demanded to know what in hell they thought they were doing and threatened severe consequences for their inexcusable behavior. The pressure of the bayonet on my navel eased a little and the officer withdrew his pistol from my back. I turned and faced him and harshly demanded an explanation.

Apologetically, he explained that he was merely following orders to shoot me on sight! Fortunately, it never dawned on him that by talking and not shooting me, he was disobeying his orders. Naturally, I didn't bring the error to his attention. Apparently there had been a riot in town the previous day (this was not surprising or unusual as the country was rapidly slipping into political anarchy at that time). A tocadequeda or curfew had been imposed by the army in order to restore order and anyone found on the street after a bugle announced the noon curfew was to be shot, no questions asked.

Still furious, I shouted that whatever had gone on was no business of mine, that these rules were for citizens and obviously did not apply to me. They could see I was a tourist — I had a camera. They could see I was not a Colombian, but a North American who had just come to visit their beautiful town. This was no way to treat important tourists such as myself!

The officer abjectly apologized. Having taken full control of the situation, I continued to glare angrily at him for another moment. Then, after taking a deep breath, I graciously forgave him and conceded that I could now understand his error due to his surprise at my sudden arrival. Then, believe it or not, I complimented him on how fast and efficiently he and his men had reacted and surrounded me. He smiled gratefully as he holstered his gun. The sergeant removed his bayonet from my navel and the other soldiers pointed their bayonets to the ground.

"You may have been surprised at my arrival, but I was even more startled by yours!" I laughed. The whole platoon grinned back and laughed. We then exchanged the customary elaborate Spanish compliments — expressing our admiration for each other, acknowledging each other's bravery, courage and courtesy, and expressing our patriotic love of Colombia and Canada and our countries' great friendship for each other.

I explained that my wife and two friends were on another street. I stated I would find them and that we would then leave their beautiful town immediately. After an aristocratic nod to the men, which they gratefully acknowledged, and a condescending handshake with the officer who glowed with appreciation at my generous gesture, I turned and walked away, praying that they would still fail to realize they had disobeyed orders and remedy the situation by shooting me in the back.

Fortunately, my wife and friends had not gone far and, at the urgency of my shouts, came running. We sped out of town into the countryside. As I recounted my experience, I realized that, had I acted in any other way or taken any other course of action, I would have been killed. I took no credit for my apparent wisdom. My unexpected behavior was a surprise even to myself.

At another time much later in my life, the same technique — doing the unexpected — again saved me from possible death or at least a severe beating.

By then, I was living in Vancouver. An interesting movie was playing at a theatre close to me and one evening I asked a lady a few years younger than my 60 years to accompany me to it. After the show, we walked the few blocks to the ocean to view the summer sunset, then strode towards my apartment building where I had left my car, in order to drive her home. Separating Stanley Park from my own and adjacent apartment buildings was a shaded four-foot walkway, and it was along here that we chose to walk in the evening dusk. Although no one else was on the walk at the time, we had no concern for our safety since Vancouver is normally a quite peaceful city with little violence.

Suddenly out of the bushes beside us jumped five very husky young men. Surrounding us, they shoved us, shouting obscenities, addressing my female companion in particularly abusive terms. I suppose the normal reaction of a man would have been to object and try to protect the lady's good name — in turn provoking an even more violent response. Instead I did the unexpected — I laughed!

I laughed, not at them, but at what they said, adopting the attitude that they were being intentionally funny and conveying the impression that I saw their shoving as a friendly gesture. They were nonplussed and, for a moment, silent.

"What the hell," one of the men finally said, "let's let these two go." One man readily agreed with him.

Keeping a friendly grin on my face, I watched the

drama unfold almost as if I were a mere spectator. The first two, after some considerable persuasion, convinced two more of their gang to let us go. But the last young man would have none of it. He again began to scream obscenities at us, his face reddening and contorting with rage. It was obvious to me that he was either on drugs or was a psychopath. He was the most muscular of the five and I realized that, at my age, there would be little I could do to protect myself in a physical encounter with him. I wondered what would next occur.

An amazing thing happened. The raving man's four companions each grabbed one of his appendages and bodily carried him away kicking and thrashing. We watched them go until they turned a corner and were out of sight, but it was some time before the sound of his angry screams and blasphemies finally faded away.

"That was a narrow escape, wasn't it?" I commented to my speechless companion. "Perhaps you'd like a cup of coffee?"

The Spiral

Papa prepares a salad for lunch which we eat on the patio. Afterwards, I remark, "You've been talking of what you've learned of things that have helped you personally. But how about the world? How about our big problems? What do we do about them? Think there's any solution?"

"Responsibility," Papa answers emphatically.

"Responsibility? Why responsibility? I expected you to say 'Peace' or 'Brotherly Love' or more understanding, something like that. Why responsibility?"

"If we learnt responsibility would we not solve all

our other problems? And is not our lack of responsibility the basic cause of those problems in the first place? Let's examine it."

On a promontory, high above the mighty Columbia River which divides the states of Oregon and Washington, stands an exact replica of Stonehenge, the mysterious monolith whose original purpose time forgot. On a nearby plaque, I read the explanation that Stonehenge marked the annual appearance of various astronomical events. Perhaps, I mused, it marked a mystery beyond that. Who erected those stones? And how? And why? What religious rites were performed there? What sacrifices were made? Or, more romantically, were they something else entirely, perhaps a monument left by visitors from outer space?

Still in a pensive mood, I turned to appreciate the marvelous panorama of river, hills and forest. Soon my attention was distracted by a large flock of small birds feeding on the tiny seeds of the low bushes hugging the river's cliff. A part of the flock, consisting of about two hundred birds, obeying some unseen signal, rose as one and flew about a hundred feet along the slope. Shortly, another segment rose and overflew the first. Then another, and yet another leapfrogged over the first two groups as the entire flock, in segments, proceeded along the bank. I fancied how much the flock resembled human society with each segment a nation and how, as with the flock, one nation might advance ahead of the others only to be overtaken in its turn.

Suddenly, obeying some instantaneous telepathic command, the whole flock rose as one and disappeared from sight. Obviously, while each bird was an individual with unique characteristics, its individuality was subservient to the psychology of the flock of which it was just a small part. The flock itself was a unit, one creature.

Man exhibits similar behavior at times.

I was once a part of a mob. I was fourteen and it was Halloween. A crowd of men prowled the city streets, caught by a growing sense of excitement and anticipation. Suddenly, a brick flew through a storefront window. With the sound of shattering glass, the crowd coalesced into a mob. We all ran in panic, rushing down the street, then flowing into a narrow dark alley. The shout of 'Police' gave even greater impetus to our blind stampede. In the mad rush, the man running in front of me stumbled over blocks of loose broken concrete. Trying to avoid him and being pushed from behind, I too lost my balance and fell heavily onto the same jagged blocks while the mob ran over me. Bleeding and with clothes torn, I regained my feet. Bordering the back alley was an eight-foot fence. After pulling myself to the top, I bent over, preparing to leap into the yard below. While in that exposed position, my departure was accelerated by a vicious swat from a policeman's billy club delivered with expertise to the appropriate spot. Safely alone from both mob and police on the far side of the fence, I realized I had done no wrong and, after wiping away the dirt and blood as best I could, I returned to the main street and waited for a streetcar to take me home.

A mob is a primitive, aboriginal creation, its members but the cells of a single body, communicating via "group think" or mental telepathy. I did not throw the brick that smashed that window, but as part of the mob, its deed was my deed; its guilt, my guilt; its fear, my fear; its panic, my panic. Lost was my sense of self and individuality. Like stampeding cattle, a mob is insane, holds only negative emotions and goals, and rushes to its own destruction. We can understand Einstein saying, "When I consider the stupidity of man, then I begin to comprehend infinity".

Mankind's history might be considered to have a

spiral configuration. Progress seems slow, the spiral tightly coiled like a spring to resemble an everlasting circle. We go round and round, continuously treading similar ground, making the same mistakes generation after generation and gaining but little wisdom from our previous follies. This tight spiral, this circle, has been apparent even within my own lifetime. I remember the illegal alcohol and debts of the roaring 20's, the depression of the dirty 30's, the warring 40's, the dull, boring 50's, the hippy 60's, the inflating, swinging 70's and the illegal drug and debt-drenched 80's. The problems of the 80's were almost the same problems as the 20's. As the circle continues, the 90's seem destined to be a depression like the 30's. (Incidentally, the ancient Mayans visualized the world in a similar circular way and measured the circumference of the circle as 55 years, which is more precise than the six decades I've described.)

Somehow we lurched through our past problems and although (as they always do) our problems today seem even bigger and more serious—wars, revolutions, torture, fanaticism, hostages, child abuse, street gangs, towering debts, drugs, alcoholism, divorce, organized crime, starvation, prostitution, to name a few—I am confident mankind will survive. But to advance along the spiral of history we must also solve these problems instead of postponing the solution and having them repeat like a circle time after time.

The solution to all our problems has always been the same—it is simply to learn to take responsibility for ourselves. Responsibility, as defined by Fritz Perls, the founder of Gestalt Therapy, is response-ability—using our ability to respond sanely and wisely to a given situation. A demand will always be satisfied. If not legally, then illegally. The drug problem today, for instance, is similar to the problems of the alcohol Prohibition days of the 20's. In both of these cases, crime became well organized to fill the demand. As it was illegal to consume liquor, like drugs today, it became 'chic', 'smart', the 'in thing' to do, and the demand increased. Then, as now, the media, declaiming the problem in editorials and headlines and film, advertised the forbidden fruit. Ever more stringent laws were passed against liquor and those that supplied it and, as with today's drug scene in North America, enormous amounts of money were spent annually in futile attempts to enforce those laws.

When drinking became legal once more, what happened to the rum runners? They were out of business, the last shipment remaining on the docks, the bootleggers forced to turn to less profitable occupations. By repealing Prohibition, the responsibility for the use or mis-use of alcohol was left to the individual. It was the simple, sane and cheap solution. Similarly, if drugs today were cheap, sold at cost, and readily available in drugstores, the organized crime syndicates would dissolve and the pushers would be unemployed, for there would be no profit in it. The individual would be responsible for his or her own drug use. Eventually, we will have to accept such a solution again. For ultimate responsibility rests, as it always has, entirely with the individual and not with "society".

Take one other example—debt. Over the last few years, the acquiring of debt has been encouraged as it was in the 20's, and the total now owed by North Americans, both personally and through our governments and corporations, can be guesstimated to exceed fifteen trillions of dollars. This debt cannot be repaid in dollars but will be repaid in suffering and hardship by borrower and lender alike, as it was in the 30's. But not everyone acquires debt. Some, standing apart from the flock and mob-think, take responsibility for themselves and remain debt free, avoiding the difficulties of the majority.

Too often we feel it is our due, our right, to have all

our wants, desires, and wishes satisfied, and satisfied immediately. When the world doesn't give us what we expect or demand, we complain that life is unfair and feel victimized and unable to cope. We prefer complaining to enjoying our life, prefer dwelling on our problems to seeking the solution. Where does salvation lie? Not by abdicating responsibility to our neighbors, our government, our unions, or our corporations. Not by placing our faith in crowds or mobs. We are unique in the animal kingdom, unique in our ability to reason independently. Our hope lies in the dignity of acting and living sanely; sanely, as responsible individuals, in a sometimes insane world. We will make errors and mistakes but they are the lessons we must learn to avoid repeating endless cycles. Prohibitions lead to crime. Debt leads to poverty. Political power leads to tyranny.

Abraham Lincoln penned the following principles:

- You cannot bring about prosperity by discouraging thrift.

- You cannot strengthen the weak by weakening the strong.

- You cannot help the wage earner by pulling down the wage payer.

- You cannot further the brotherhood of man by encouraging class hatred.

- You cannot keep out of trouble by spending more than you earn.

- You cannot build character and courage by taking away man's initiative and independence.

- You cannot help men permanently by doing what they could and should do for themselves.

How many of these truths have we learnt? How long will we take? It may take one hundred or one hundred thousand years, but learn responsibility we must, to spiral onwards to our destiny.

Chapter 9
Powers

I leave early in the morning to obtain more information on what the university offers. Then, later in the afternoon, I meet my new friend. We have dinner and go to a theatre in the evening. Not only is she attractive but she has a great sense of humour, and we discover that we have many interests in common. I make another date with her for later in the week. Yet I miss being with Papa. Our days together are going far too quickly. He seems to have missed me too for his welcoming hug on my return is even warmer than usual and, eager to please, he asks if there is anything I'd like.

"What I'd like to do is talk about powers. Earlier tonight I went to see a hypnotist put on a show. I was very impressed by what he could make members of the audience do," I answer.

"I've seen such a demonstration too. Unfortunately, the hypnotist, for laughs, too often degrades the dignity of those hypnotized. But I'm familiar with it's use in psychotherapy and healing."

"What impressed me most was the exhibition of enormous feats of strength."

"It is impressive, isn't it? And sometimes such feats occur when you're not under hypnosis. For instance . . .

The Strength of 1000

Every so often there's a report in the news about someone lifting a car or truck with his bare hands to free someone trapped underneath — or tearing off the locked door of a car to rescue someone. In war, similar fantastic feats of strength are sometimes demonstrated and such mighty deeds are considered heroic and the hero is awarded honors and medals. We still read tales of the Viking "berserks" — the Norse warriors who fought in a wild frenzy — and such TV series as "The Incredible Hulk" are based on this phenomenon. This super-human strength manifests itself when a person's rage exceeds simple anger. He acts in a seething fury, with no consideration of risk. Afterwards, he is as dumbfounded by his display of strength as other witnesses to the occurrence.

I once had such an experience myself. I was in hospital for a delicate operation on my arm, so delicate that my body had to be completely immobilized since any minor twitch or tremor on my part could affect the success of the surgery. After I had been placed on the operating table, thick four-inch-wide webbings were strapped across my chest, hips and thighs and my good arm pinned against my body. The arm to be operated on was similarly imprisoned by yet another set of straps and only my head and toes were free.

My incarceration complete, the anesthetist placed a mask over my nose and mouth and began to anesthetize me with ether. I had had previous operations and enjoyed the ether "trip" I'd experienced. But this time was different.

"You're giving me too much, too fast," I complained. "I can't breathe, I'm suffocating."

Receiving no answer, I repeated, as simply and clearly as I could, "I can't breathe! I'm choking! Please, I don't mind taking the ether, but give it to me a little slower. I'm suffocating."

I heard a cold, professional voice say, "He's almost out, just another minute."

Rage suddenly possessed me — an uncontrolled fury at their apparent lack of caring and sheer callousness. I'd been pleasant, polite with my request, logical in my appeal and received no consideration. Enraged beyond tolerance, I sat up! The webbings broke, with loud snaps, from around my chest, thighs and arms, and I swung a wild hook with my good arm, connecting with someone's face.

Everyone present grabbed me, but were unable to push me down. Still in a cold fury, I repeated my complaint, slowly and distinctly enunciating each word, and then offered to cooperate, if they agreed to administer the ether more slowly. A nurse, wiser than all the rest, replied in a soft, soothing voice, "Okay, just lie down. We'll give it to you very slowly. It's okay. Just lie back."

The operation resumed but it came as no surprise that it was unsuccessful. I don't know who I hit when I blindly swung my fist, but the doctor was very cold and distant to me thereafter.

I had been more unconscious than conscious when I exhibited that wild feat of strength. Such feats, which are readily demonstrated under hypnotic suggestion, make me wonder what techniques of the mind might allow us to exhibit such strength on a regular basis, in our normal day-to-day existence.

We know not all we can do. We but vaguely glimpse what we are. Our potential cannot be touched or tasted, it exists in our undiscovered self. How can we bring forth that which is hidden and unknown — our power — our love — our creativity? My only suggestion is: follow your passion and ecstasy. Then what is invisible, shall become visible. Then we shall know what we really are.

The Mustard Seed

"I wonder, Papa, where these powers come from?"

"It doesn't 'come from' at all. It is always here and everywhere. Let me clarify what I'm trying to say. I don't subscribe to solipsism, the philosophy that only I, the self, exists. Obviously creation is beyond numbering. All, however, is an expression of the One, the Great Spirit. When we are gifted to see as It sees, at that moment there is only the 'I'. When in touch with It, our power knows no limits. Let me illustrate . . .

Recently, in a reverie, my consciousness drifted far beyond my body until I seemed to float in the void, to be suspended in space, the earth revolving slowly below me, like the most valuable of rare jewels on display upon the black velvet of starry space. I studied its many fascinating facets as it turned — the pure white of the clouds and icy poles, the blue of the oceans, the faint sheen of the atmosphere, the kaleidoscope of colors reflecting from the continents with their plains, rivers, lakes and mountains. While contemplating this most wondrous planet, the words of a Biblical prophecy came to mind:

"If you have faith as a mustard seed, you will say to this mountain: Move from here to there and it will move and nothing will be impossible to you."

I thought — I have faith, greater than a mustard seed, that smallest of seeds. With this thought, power surged through me. I knew I could move mountains and rearrange the world. I could do anything. This could be fun!

Leisurely, I studied the mountains. Should I push Mount Everest down? Or raise it even higher? Should I cast a mountain into the sea? Which one would I move first and where would I move it?

Slowly it dawned on me that there was no point in re-arranging mountains, for each mountain was already in its perfect place, each river flowed its perfect course, and all things had already been arranged perfectly. Then I remembered that, of course, all were in their perfect order — "I" had arranged the world that way in the first place —

The Findings

"What triggers power? What I mean is, is there a common factor that activates it and why do extraordinary powers manifest at some time and not at others?"

"Good question, Robert. It's something I've thought about quite a lot and have concluded it's great motivation, unobstructed motivation."

"Motivation? You mean if I have some sort of motive, great powers will come to my assistance?"

"Hardly. One has to want it so strongly every other consideration is ignored. One has to have tunnel vision — a one-pointed desire where nothing else matters. Think of the examples we've talked about. In every case, there is an intense need, desire or want that excludes everything else. Its the image of a man madly rushing into the raging inferno of a burning building to rescue his child and emerging unscathed."

"So all we need is great motivation?"

"Motivation that is unobstructed, unobstructed by fears or any other concerns. This is the magic of silence for in deep silence fears have no existence. Other words for this motivation are willpower or strength of will"

"Would motivation or willpower explain miraculous healings?"

"Exactly," Papa agrees. "A psychic healer told me three ingredients were needed for a healing:

- *The intense desire, willpower or motivation of the patient to be healed.*
- *The universal power.*
- *The healer to act as a conduit and focuser of that power.*

The first thing he always asked a patient was, 'Why do you want to live?' Unless he got a satisfactory answer, determining that there was sufficient motivation, he dismissed the patient explaining that he could not help. His success ratio with the others was almost 100%. I've witnessed instantaneous remissions of cancer, the disappearance of bleeding wounds, and many other healings. Apparent miracles."

"Can you give me another example? Some other kind of power you experienced?" I inquire.

"A few people seem to possess a special knack or gift for finding things—not only lost items but for discovering the new. Even in my chosen profession of geology, which is dedicated to finding fresh deposits of petroleum and minerals, rare indeed are the finders. Although successful in discovering several deposits, I did not realize how unusual that talent really was until, on a summer vacation, I discovered my ability to find lost possessions."

"Would you tell me about it?" I request.

"The motivation for what happened was not my motivation. The intense desire came from another. Nevertheless, great motivation was present, and I was the conduit for the power. A woman had lost something of great value but could not find her possession herself for worries and fears and sadness over the loss nullified her motivation and obstructed the flow of power through her."

"What exactly happened?" I ask.

The beach at Oyster River on Vancouver Island was a mile-long arc of perfection with our rented cabin right at its edge, so that we stepped directly from cottage to sand. The beach itself was almost a thousand feet wide at low tide and, as the tidal waters crept up it on a hot summer's day, it permitted delightful sand-warmed swimming. Bordering the shoreline was a multi-stranded necklace of huge logs, some in excess of five feet in diameter, the remnants of the previous winters' storms. These logs provided a series of routes for playing "follow the leader" with my four children following and laughing behind me in descending order of age.

One afternoon, as I lay stretched out lazily in the

sunshine in front of our cottage, a small group of beach-attired vacationers walked past me, comforting an hysterically sobbing middle-aged woman in their midst. On inquiring, I learned that she had lost her wedding ring in the sand and had no idea where to look for it, as she had walked back and forth the full extent of the beach.

"Make yourself a cup of tea," I heard a very confident voice say. "And take it easy. I'll go and get your ring!"

With a feeling akin to horror, I recognized that voice. It was my own! What possessed me to say such an idiotic thing? How was I supposed to find her ring? It was impossible. "Well, how are you going to get out of this one?", I asked myself.

At my words, some small hope had gleamed in the distraught woman's eyes and her wailing diminished. Summoning what little confidence I had and under the intense stares of her friends, who obviously thought I was some kind of nut, I marched bravely onto the beach.

My heart sank when I saw the view before me. It was low tide. Five million square feet of sand and pebbles lay exposed. Somewhere in that expanse a ring, half an inch in diameter, was hiding. The beach was filled with people — walking, running, playing games or just sitting. One misplaced step by any of these sun lovers and the lost ring would be buried forever.

I turned to the right and proceeded along an erratic, zigzag course up and down the beach. The futility of it all became even more apparent as I thought about what I was trying to do. After some time, I reversed my direction, but without hope. The proverbial needle in a haystack would be easier to find than a gold ring in golden sand, I thought. The haystack was at least in one place while this beach seemed to stretch on forever.

I finally concluded that finding the ring was an

impossibility, but how could I return to that woman empty handed? And how could I have put myself in such a ridiculous and embarrassing predicament in the first place? After 20 minutes of self- chastisement, while continuing a half-hearted search, I concluded, "You said it. You said you'd find it. So how are you going to do it?"

Obviously, there was no rational or intellectual way to keep my promise, so I decided to approach it from a non-rational, non- intellectual angle. I issued stern commands to myself,

"Brain, stop directing!"

"Feet, take me to the ring!"

"Eycs, see the ring!"

"Hands, pick it up!"

Then, with my mind stilled, I allowed my feet to go where they wished. My erratic wandering became a direct path and finally, as I approached the far end of the beach, my feet stopped moving. Before me lay the ring, half-buried in the sand.

When I returned the prized item to its delighted owner, as nonchalantly as possible, she and her friends naturally expressed their astonishment at my success. But deep down, nobody was more surprised or amazed than me.

I'm sure you would think that I might have learned a lesson from that experience — to keep my mouth shut, if nothing else. But, no, not me. One winter's evening a few years later, my wife and I went to the Petroleum Club to have dinner. While waiting in the foyer for my wife's return from the cloakroom, a couple I knew — good friends — came through the door.

"Hi, Doc!" I greeted the man and we cordially shook hands. "Nice to see you, Em," I said, turning to his wife. Then, noticing a look of obvious distress on her face, I asked, "What's the matter? Are you alright?"

She explained that she had just lost a diamond earring. "I know I had it when I left home, but when we arrived here, it was gone. We went back and searched the car, but it's not there," she blurted out with a few fearful, sidelong glances at her angry husband. "So it can only have fallen off between the car and the club. We've walked back and forth several times, but we just can't find it. It must be lost in the snow."

"Don't worry about it," I heard myself say. "I'll go find it. Just take it easy."

Immediately I felt like kicking myself in the you-know-where. How presumptuous could I be? Why couldn't my mouth stay shut and avoid putting me into these embarrassing situations? Not waiting to get my overcoat, I headed outside. What a marvellous winter's night! Huge thick snowflakes fell lazily, filling the air with sparkling stars and making fluffy piles of diamonds underfoot. The landscape glistened. Traffic noise was hushed. I was alone in a holy, crystal cathedral.

How was I to find one small diamond in this world of diamonds? Remembering my experience with the gold ring in the golden sand at Oyster River, I repeated what I had done then. I stilled my mind, commanded my feet to take me to the earring and ordered my hands to pick it up. I didn't tell my eyes to see it — it would be invisible under the soft piles of fresh snow.

Walking leisurely about three-quarters of the way to the open parking lot, I stopped just once. I stooped and the snow melted against my probing fingers as I picked up the tiny diamond earring. Before returning, I stood for another moment looking at the sky and, as the snow fell and melted on my face, I gave a "thank you" for the wonder and the magic — the wonder of my finding and the magic of the night.

I received effusive words of gratitude as I returned the earring. "No problem!" I lied.

Blow-out

When my life has been at risk, has some Power protected, preserved me? Is there a Power that watches over each of us? I believe that such a Power exists, and that the love of life is that Power. When the soul wearies of life, we die. As long as our spirit is filled with enthusiasm, eagerness and laughter we will keep on living. Let me give you an example of how my life was preserved—-

Long weary of winter, residents of northern communities await the coming of spring with intense anticipation. Often, in those towns located on rivers, lotteries are organized, with the winnings awarded to the person who guesses closest to the exact time and day of spring "break up," when the winter's ice breaks apart and the river becomes navigable again. With the development of increasingly precise technology, sophisticated electronic devices have been invented to record the exact instant of this auspicious event.

Spring breakup heralds many changes — the re-awakening of the earth and the approaching season of planting and plowing; spring house cleaning; a change of clothing from heavy parkas and boots to the lighter, less restrictive wear of spring and summer; and a renewal of the spirit, a time of jubilation.

It was also the signal for oil exploration crews to cease operations in the north. There, exploration could only be carried out while the ground was frozen and heavy trucks were able to travel across the terrain on trails cut by bulldozers through the muskeg and scrub forest. With spring these primitive roads became impassable and any vehicle reckless enough to attempt them, hopelessly mired. As the ground thawed and roads turned to mush, the Department of Highways also imposed travel bans on all highways for heavy vehicles. During the 1950's, spring breakup and road-ban times were a matter of vital concern to me and my geophysical exploration crews. It was important to work as long as possible in the north and then escape just before these road bans were imposed, so as not to be trapped and unable to continue our exploration activity in the drier south.

In mid-March of 1956, I visited one of my crews in the Peace River country to review their work progress and to check to ensure they would be able to leave immediately, once the official warning of the imminent road-ban had been issued. However, the weather which had been warm enough to shrink the piled snows to a fraction of their former size, was turning cold again, the 30 degree below zero temperature ensuring a delay in road bans for several days. My work completed late on the third afternoon, I then decided to travel home to Calgary almost 500 miles away (I did crazy things like that in those days).

Like the other few roads in that country, the highway was a graded two-lane track, constructed by piling the dirt from the bordering ditches into the center. Over the mud, like thin icing on a cake, was a coat of gravel which promptly disappeared when the rains turned the earth to ooze and the road to ruts. In winter, traffic compressed the snows to form a hard surface of rough ice. This narrow road — Alberta's Provincial Highway 2, at the time — twisted through scrub pines between lakes, swamps and muskeg.

It was after midnight as I drove my car past the village of Lesser Slave Lake. All was in darkness, even the gas station. A dozen miles or so further down the road, I discovered that a warm rain had previously fallen and formed a slick icy surface on the road — suddenly I was on a skating rink eleven feet wide and a hundred miles long! I slowed to a safer 15 miles an hour and considered my options. Obviously I had no good alternative but to proceed. The road was so narrow that I doubted if I could turn my car around to find shelter and, in any case, there was nothing to go back to as even the small motel I had seen in Lesser Slave Lake had no lights on and was either closed or full. I couldn't stop and wait for morning when there would be traffic and help. I'd be frozen long before sunup. Safety, shelter and fuel all lay over a hundred miles ahead.

I continued my journey, sometimes accelerating dangerously to 25 miles an hour on the straight stretches and spinning the steering wheel as the car slipped from side to side and skidded from icy rut to icy rut. Twisting curves were negotiated in wild arcs, at 10 to 15 miles an hour.

Time passed slowly. My shoulders ached with tension and the rapid turning of the wheel as I fought to compensate for the skidding. I was conscious of the falling temperature outside as the car itself became cold, although the heater was operating at maximum. My bones were chilled.

I travelled through a glistening canyon formed by the reflection of the icy road surface in the car's headlights and framed by the foreboding black of the stunted pines and never ending muskeg on either side. I became one with the car, reacting automatically to each skid, swerve and skew. Alone. No other car or truck had been seen for three hours and I figured it would be at least 10:00 or 11:00 the following morning before anyone else ventured that way.

It was about 3:00 am when it happened. Suddenly I became aware that the car was slowing, that my foot was off the gas. What had possessed me to slow down unconsciously like that, I wondered. And what was now restraining me from accelerating again? At this point, the car was barely crawling along at five miles an hour.

At that instant, with a bang, a front tire blew out! The car skidded, out of control. Desperately , I spun the steering wheel this way and that. Miraculously and to my intense relief, my vehicle remained on the road. Had I been travelling at any higher speed, the car would have skidded into the ditch and been impossible to extricate. The gasoline supply would have been insufficient to keep the car warm for many more hours and I would have frozen to death long before anyone passed that way to offer help.

As it was, I changed the blown tire for the spare and carried on, eventually refuelling at the village of Westlock and, as the freezing rain had not fallen that far south, proceeding to the city of Edmonton, 45 miles away. I arrived at 7:30 a.m., as a blood-red dawn broke through the storm-splintered sky. At my brother's home I borrowed a couch for a few hours of exhausted sleep before continuing my journey to Calgary.

What had made me slow the car? I was not even conscious of taking my foot off the gas. What intuition, what clairvoyance, what Power had saved my life? I had no answers to these questions, but gratefully accepted my gift of life.

Silence

I brew a pot of decaffeinated coffee and set out a plate of cookies. Refreshed, I comment, "Papa, I've noticed how much you're silent. You talk easily enough when you've something to say but you don't engage in much small talk. Not that I mind, silence with you is comfortable, but it is unusual. Most people seem to dread silence and fill their world with sound—talking, radio, and television. I think that silence to you is not just an absence of sound, but something more — almost like a power that you use."

"Right you are, Robert."

Silence is not just the cessation of talk, the lack of noise, nor is it a mere quietude of body and mind. It is all those, of course, but deep silence is so much more. It's something tangible. Silence is the home of power. It is the state of maximum potential out of which all things are created. Going into silence is like going into a tunnel. Its end is beyond time and space where ultimate reality resides.

Silence can be employed at both the spiritual level and pragmatically in our day-to-day experiences with other people, as I first discovered when dealing with government. My company had purchased a petroleum lease with an abandoned well on it. Studying the data I decided the well had been poorly completed and that substantial quantities of oil and gas still remained. The problem was that the lease was burdened with an excessive royalty and the economics were such that the risk of the cost of a re-completion could not be justified.

I arranged a meeting with the government where I disclosed all my data and stated the problem. The Minister listened carefully and then informed me other companies had made similar requests to reduce the royalty on other leases but the government policy had been decided. No change in the terms of any lease would be allowed.

Smiling and stating that I understood, I asked, "So how are *WE* going to accomplish what I want?"

The Minister opened his mouth as if to say something, closed it again, and then just stared at me, waiting for me to communicate further.

Sitting comfortably, with a friendly expression on my face, I became silent and went into the quiet depth of my being. Minutes passed. The Minister looked perplexed, then uncomfortable and, finally, he looked thoughtful. More time passed. Silence became tangible. "Well", he said, clearing his voice, "We could destroy the old lease and I could sell you a new one carrying the normal amount of royalty. Mind you, though, you'd have to guarantee to carry out the recompletion of the well."

"That will be just fine," I said immediately, standing up and shaking his hand. In due course, the well was successfully re-completed and produced oil, gas and profit for both my company and the government, and may still be producing to this day.

The power of deep silence manifests in many ways. One's reaction time is swift and one's response or action is invariably right and life supporting. To illustrate:

After an intense ten-day meditative retreat, I met my wife and together we drove along the narrow two-lane highway to the city of Victoria. At one point there was a line of about 20 cars speeding in the opposite direction when suddenly a car at the end of that line cut into my lane. At the high speeds we were both travelling, there was but a second before impact.

Without braking, I steered the car into the deep ditch. Allowing the threatening car to pass, I then gunned the engine to regain the road once more, barely avoiding a bridge which crossed the ditch into a farmyard. I had been talking quietly before the emergency and continued to calmly speak throughout the incident. The entire event took less time than I've taken to tell about it. Only after regaining the road did my wife begin to scream in fear. Undisturbed, my heartbeat and breathing remained even and calm, my mind serene.

The power of silence is well known and accepted in Hindu and Buddhist religions and a Mauni, one who remains in continuous meditative silence, is recognized as a powerful guru or teacher. Originally Jesus taught meditation as attested to by the writings of the early church Fathers (see "The Philokalia" and "The Art of Prayer", translated by Kadlonbovsky and Palmer.) However, until recently, the technique of meditation, the skill to achieve this deep silence, has been lost to our western religious culture. On the other hand, the Greek Catholic church has kept the meditative tradition alive, at least until lately (see "The Way of a Pilgrim", translated by R.M. French). As meditation techniques were re-introduced to Europe and the Americas by various eastern gurus, Christian churches began to advertise courses in "Christian" meditation. As meditation itself is something natural, the phrase "Christian Meditation" makes as much sense as "Christian Sleep" or "Christian Bowel Movements".

One might reasonably assume that monks in monasteries who spend hours in contemplative solitude would be familiar with the power of silence. This is not the case. When asked what they do during their required times of meditation, contemplation or solitude, as they variously refer to it, they reply, "Oh, I say a bunch of Hail Marys, recite Prayers, read my Bible, and sometimes just sit and try to reach God." Inquiring what results are achieved, a frequent reply is, "I get a headache".

The power of silence can be used destructively like fire, nuclear or any other power. Some couples, when angry, indulge in its negative use by not speaking to each other. The Power of Silence works and energy accumulates until it explodes with yelling, screaming, or violence. In the same way, when workers ostracize a fellow employee by not speaking to him or associating with him, he invariably quits. We are gregarious animals and expulsion from society is a deadly punishment. In the early days in America, when traders lived in forts, the punishment for a serious crime was expulsion without weapons or supplies. A slow, lonely death resulted. As John Donne once said, "No man is an island," and rare indeed is the man who thinks he can live entirely alone without assistance.

I personally experienced being ostracized while living in a Benedictine monastery for a month and a half. The monks under the rules of St. Benedict are forbidden to talk to outsiders other than to greet them politely and briefly. I was excluded from all their activities other than meals and their five daily religious ceremonies which consisted primarily of Gregorian chanting.

Meals too were eaten in silence, except for prayers

and one monk reading aloud from a book. Their choice of reading materials was interesting. The first such book that I heard read was quite appropriate to the surroundings. It was "Recent Happenings in England" recounting the difficulties that Anselmo, the Archbishop of Canterbury, was having with William the Conqueror and his son Henry I in the latter part of the 11th century. It chronicled the struggle between church and royalty as to who was boss. The monks smiled when the church was winning.

During meal times, the monks sat in a square with their backs to the wall, the dining tables in front of them. In the exact center of the room, as far away from the monks as possible was a small table with four chairs. That's where I ate my meals, usually in solitary splendor, occasionally with other guests, and sometimes with the guest master who hospitably served me with such food as he judged generously sufficient.

A time of quietude I had desired and expected. Isolation from normal social intercourse I had not. I doubt if I could have tolerated it for long had not a priest arrived who was taking a personal retreat to finalize his decision to leave the priesthood. Not being a monk, he was free to talk. We became friends and found we had many interests in common.

Getting into the monastery at all had required using the power of silence. The guest master was pleased that I wished to come for a retreat. But when I informed him that I wanted to stay for six weeks, his reaction was unexpected.

"Impossible! It can't be done. No one has ever stayed so long before. A priest came once for four weeks but he left every weekend. So you see, it's impossible."

Remembering my experience a few years previously with the Deputy Minister, I said, "I understand how impossible it is and yet I know you understand my desire to come for six weeks. Now what are WE going to do about it?"

Then I dropped into deep silence. Again the reaction was curious. He fidgeted, opened his mouth to speak, closed it again, half stood, then sat down again. Finally, he appealed to the Abbot who hospitably agreed to my request.

Chapter 10
Questions Not Quite Answered

"What I'm wondering about, Papa, is how come you've had so many strange experiences? What makes you different?"

"Oh, I don't think I'm different," he laughs, "I think everyone has both psychic and spiritual experiences."

"But you've had so many —"

"It seems to me that there's a human tendency to perceive the universe neatly ruled into comfortable little squares and cubes. Most people don't want to be disturbed by what doesn't fit into their cubicle. So they ignore the strange, write their experiences off as dreams or coincidences and shut them out of their memory. I'm fascinated and excited by the unusual and always want to learn more. Perhaps I'm just a little more open to accepting these things."

"Would you tell me more about your mystical or spiritual experiences? How much credence do you give them? And how much could be imagination, or a heightened daydream, something like that?" I ask.

"At those times I know I glimpse a reality far beyond the day-to-day world we live in. Like in Plato's cave analogy, our ordinary world is but the flickering shadows cast on the cave-walls of our ignorance while hidden from our sight and beyond our usual comprehension is the fire-light of reality. When I see that light and experience that reality I cannot doubt it. I may doubt other people, doubt they even exist. I may doubt the world, doubt it even exists. I may doubt myself, doubt I even exist. I may doubt anything and everything. But That, That I cannot ever doubt. I may not understand. I cannot doubt.

"What don't you understand? I thought you understood just about everything. What is it that you don't understand?"

"There's quite a bit I don't understand," he grins and then becomes serious . . .

Non-Duality

Most of the deep mystical experiences I've had follow a consistent pattern. Typically, there is an opening, a giving-way, a going far beyond—beyond thought, body, the world. Then there is Light, which St. Augustine described as a Light not of this world—a flooding of Light—a pouring of shining glory—rays upon rays, flashes upon flashes ever brightening—until I merge and meld, dissolving into that Light. I am no more. There is only Light. There are no words for it. There is no time, no life, no right, no wrong, no separateness. Only Light, radiating a perfect happiness, where Light and Love are synonymous.

These experiences reveal the glory of the spiritual realm and the truth that all is a sublime unity, an eternal Am-ness. There is no duality; all is one. Buddhists call this knowledge of oneness the Doctrine of Non-Duality. But how quickly this knowledge is lost. How easily is duality re-incorporated. I decide to buy a shirt. Will I purchase the white one or the blue—or perhaps the yellow? I make choices and exercise judgement. This will look better than that, it will better complement my other clothes. Day-to-day life is a continuous series of decisions, choices and judgements. Think how many decisions and judgements and choices we make while driving a car! Realizing there are choices, we live with a myriad of dualities and the sense of the One is lost. Continuously and of necessity we choose that this is right, proper, injurious, sinful, likable, distasteful, safe or dangerous. We judge our government, churches, unions, business, others, ourselves, even the weather. Where is the remembrance that all these are One? Lao-Tsu, the originator of Taoism, with his gentle humor said this of duality:

Tao is without difficulty!
Only avoid picking and choosing,
Worry and judgement,
Striving and wanting,
Liking and disliking!
A split-hair difference
Sets heaven and earth apart!

Duality, he continued, requires that to balance good there's bad; for beauty, there is ugliness; for good government, misrule; for kindness, brutality. Duality is a sickness of the mind, a feverish illusion. Non-Duality—no up or down, no in or out, no before or after, no thing or doing—that is the Tao, the Truth, the Reality.

I doubt if one can live in the world without duality, without making choices. And those who try must surely retreat to a barren cave, preferably without even a loin cloth, and eat or drink only as some good Samaritan provides. I know "Oneness" on a level that is beyond questioning, where there is no room for doubt. Yet I am a human in this world, with desires and appetites, urges and wants, this place where duality is ever present. Does not being human mean to be aware of duality and our ability to choose and make changes? — to comfort a loved one and dry their tears — to encourage a child — to heal the wounds of the injured — to feed a brother who hungers?

I cannot entirely resolve this quandary or paradox. Perhaps the magnet provides a helpful symbol for it has dual opposing poles and it needs that duality to exist as one magnet. So I live, knowing Non-Duality, while still enjoying this marvellous magnetic Duality.

Guadeloupe

In 1949, leisurely returning to Canada after two and half years in South America, my wife and I spent several days in Mexico City. The high mountain air was sweet, the streets clean and the people friendly. Our two-room suite and bath in the newest luxury hotel cost less than $4 per day while $10 allowed us to hire a taxi driven by a government-approved guide for a tour of the pyramids and the many other outlying places of interest.

We were tired as we drove back to the city. Sunset was near. It had been a long day. Our guide informed us that we had one more important stop — the Shrine of Guadeloupe. I told him we were weary and just wished to return to the hotel, that we were not really interested. I had seen enough shrines during my time in Colombia and the customary piles of crutches and testimonials at such places did not impress me. I had no use for plaster saints, even those that supposedly wept. The guide assured us that the shrine was on our way and would take little time. He then proceeded to tell the following story:

> Not many years after the Spanish conquest, a miracle occurred. The Virgin Mary appeared to a peasant in the countryside and instructed him to go to the Bishop and tell him She wished to have a church built at that exact spot. He did as commanded but naturally the Bishop did not believe his story.
>
> A few days later, the Mother of God again appeared to the peasant and demanded to know where Her church was. Informed of what the Bishop had said, She instructed him to return once more and demand Her church be built. This he did and again the Bishop refused to believe, demanding proof.
>
> Again the Virgin Mary appeared to the peasant in the field and again She asked where Her church was and again he explained what had happened. She then told him to go to a certain hillside and pick the flowers that were growing there and to

> present the bouquet to the Bishop. Also he was to give his cloak to the church dignitary.
>
> When the Bishop received the flowers he realized something unusual was occurring for the flowers were long out of season. Told the complete story once more, he believed. Then the peasant took his cloak off and gave it to the Bishop. A portrait of Mary, Herself, was miraculously found on the inside of the garment. The cloak, made from the untreated fibres of the Century plant, should have decayed to dust within a few years but the miracle continued. The picture remained bright and the cloak did not deteriorate although almost 400 years had now passed. When the church was built, innumerable miracles and healings occurred. It was and still is the most revered spot in all Mexico.

By the time we arrived at the Shrine, our three year old daughter had fallen asleep and my wife, convalescing from an illness, said she wished to remain and rest in the taxi. Inside the church, the guide showed me the solid gold altar, the various jewelled plaques on the walls from grateful recipients of the Virgin's favours and the usual piles of crutches and written testimonials. From the high dome in the centre hung an enormous gold crown studded with huge gems which glowed softly in the dusk. The guide claimed that if the church was ever destroyed, the value of the crown alone would be sufficient to rebuild it, solid gold altar and all.

Left alone, I sat in a rear pew. Silence absorbed me. Shortly I sensed a Presence, a Power, and over me swept both a deep peace and a feeling of infinite compassion. My soul disturbed, my disbelief was shaken.

End of story. The end, that is, until 38 years later when I again visited Mexico City. This time smog polluted the air and the streets were filled with refuse and beggars. Now the cost of a taxi and a personal guide was prohibitive. Price dictated that sightseeing be done by tour bus. On such a tour we stopped to visit a typical Spanish church dwarfed by the enormous stone platform on which it was centered. That platform had been the floor of an ancient Aztec temple razed by the Conquistadores. Fascinated, I spent most of the allotted time investigating the ruin and entered the church but briefly, noting its one unusual feature — a huge mural that covered the far wall depicting an Indian standing in a field of artificial-looking flowers.

While travelling to our next stop, the Shrine of Guadeloupe, the guide told a similar story to the one I had previously heard, explaining further that the peasant in the church mural was the peasant of the legend and that recently he had been beatified and was now a saint. The church we had just visited was very holy, he stated, for the saint had attended it as a child.

Arriving at the Shrine, I discovered it was now a beautiful modernistic church, not the church of my memory. The guide pointed out to me the old church which was sinking into the soft soil of the lake-bed on which Mexico City was built. It had a decided list. He further explained that my remembered church had not been the original shrine and pointed out a third church which had sunk even further. I was disappointed that entrance to both old churches was forbidden, being considered dangerous.

Although hundreds of people milled near the entrance to the Shrine, there was a hush, broken only by the shouts from hawkers of religious souvenirs. Tightly packed, we were herded into an anteroom of the church. Railings led onto a moving walkway which traversed its length. High on the wall facing us, brightly flood-lit and ornately framed was the miracle of the peasant's cloak with its miraculous portrait.

But what was I looking at? A garish full-bodied

painting of a man with a long white beard, stiffly seated on a golden throne. He was richly garbed in a scarlet gown, an oversized crown on his head like the crown I had seen in the old church. A portrait with no artistic merit. A cheap stylized version of the King of Heaven. I felt a faint repugnance. That in no way depicted my concept of God. Maybe it was the concept of ignorant superstitious peasants — but it sure wasn't mine.

But wait! Wasn't it supposed to be a picture of Mary? Was I seeing right? I rubbed my eyes, blinked, shook my head. The picture remained bright and clear. Yet was I seeing what others were seeing?

I stumbled as the sidewalk ended and, pushed from behind, stepped onto the returning moving walkway to transverse the room once more. By now I was more than half convinced I was seeing something not there. I tried to force an image of Mary into my mind. Vaguely in the shadows behind the King of Heaven, I imagined that I could discern a Rubinesque Madonna and Child but guessed again I saw as others did not.

The sidewalk ended and I was carried along by the crowd into the church. Suddenly undefined emotions engulfed me. I began to weep. My eyes flowed, my nose ran. I could not control my flood of tears and the great sobs which shook my body. Gratefully I accepted a package of Kleenex from a companion. The visit over but still sobbing, blindly I was led back to the bus. The guide nodded and assured me, "It often happens."

Later I learned my suspicions were true. The miraculous picture was a simple bust of Mary — no King, no throne, no shadowy mother, no infant child. I had not seen the miracle that was there. Mine was another miracle. But a miracle of what or for what? I could not even clearly define the spectrum of emotions I had felt while weeping other than some embarrassment at my emotional display.

A wistful anguish, a compassionate longing had possessed me. But for what? What had my miracle been given to teach? Facing my own arrogance, I admitted that a peasant's simple faith was greater than mine. A simple faith that believed in all miracles.

Perhaps the tears were to wash my arrogance away. And perhaps I wept in compassion for all of us.

Chapter 11
Wildness

"I dreamt about you last night, Papa."

"A pleasant dream, I hope?"

"Very. In my dream you were huge, enormously strong, like a Paul Bunyan, dressed for the wilderness in a bright red checked shirt open to expose a hairy chest. Over the earth you strode in mile-long strides. Then in my dream you stopped, bent down to let your mighty fingers probe deep into the rocky soil. Glowing gems were extracted. Tenderly you placed them in my hands. Time and again you repeated the procedure until the abundance overflowed my grasp. I recognize the dream for what it was and thank you for your gifts."

He bows slightly and with a smile asks, "So what color gem would you like today?"

"After my dream, I'm eager to hear more about your adventures when you explored for oil and minerals in far corners of the world. Perhaps you, your generation, saw the last of the world's wilderness."

"I think we did, and it's unfortunate for, as Henry Thoreau said, 'In wildness is the preservation of the world.'"

"What do you exactly mean by wildness, Papa?"

"Wildness in nature is wilderness 'untamed'. Wildness in man is the spirit untamed. As Henry Thoreau once asked: How many of us lead lives of quiet desperation? Desperate lives where wildness is enslaved? What fences have we erected and what walls have we built to protect ourselves? Those walls imprison us. Of course there is a risk in breaking out of our comfort zone, the supposed safety of the familiar, but if we do not risk, we miss life itself.

"My life has been at risk many times," Papa

continues. "Dealing with peril, successfully overcoming the crisis, is the spice of life. With it comes a feeling of exhilaration — of truly being alive. Few drink deeply from the cup of life. Some sip suspiciously. The rest merely gargle loudly."

"We should try to risk our lives?" I ask.

"Of course not. We must use our common sense but we should experience life's excitement in spite of danger and risk."

"Common sense? You seem to have always relied on more spiritual powers."

"Guess I've been talking mostly about the unusual —— they make interesting stories —— but both the material and spiritual components in life are important. Both intuition and common sense are tools we can employ to remedy our problems. However, when my life was at risk, just employing knowledge, skill, and common sense usually got me out of those difficulties. Let me give you an example or two from my days in the wilderness. . . .

Fire

Exploring regions of the world far beyond the bounds of civilization may seem romantic and incredibly exciting. The mundane truth, however, is that living in such areas is simply boring, for the most part.

After the day's tasks are done, what is there to entertain? You can listen to the radio, music and voices from far away; play a game of cards; engage in idle chitchat with co-workers who are as weary of you as you are of them; or write home and dream of a reunion with sorely missed loved ones. If you're brave enough, or not too exhausted, you might take a solitary walk in the night wilderness. The monotony is rarely broken — but when it is, the interruptions are usually both dramatic and violent.

In the months of Arctic night, the greatest danger

is fire. If fire destroys one's shelter, death by freezing follows. My accommodation in the winter of 1945/46 was a sleigh, 17 feet long and 7 feet wide. The camp, a miniature village, consisted of ten such bunk sleighs for sleeping, two for cooking and eating, and nine for supplies and equipment. These sleighs in sets of four were towed by bulldozers from one location to the next as we mapped the sub-surface geology of the area. The bunk sleighs, accommodating eight men each, had double walls and triple floors for protection from the subzero temperatures which hovered between 50 and 60 degrees below. Heating was by means of a converted oil barrel laid on its side with a door for loading wood. The chopped logs were both frozen and green, and only produced heat once they were blazing furiously — usually with the help of diesel fuel liberally poured over them. The diesel ignited with explosions of varying force occasionally setting a sleigh on fire. I became a rather skilled fireman over the course of the long winter and luckily only two sleighs were completely destroyed.

Always, far from civilization, fire is a great danger. In the summer of 1943, I explored and mapped an area north of Yellowknife in the Northwest Territories for the Geological Survey of Canada. One night our sleep was abruptly broken by the smell of smoke and the crackling of fire. The food supply and cook tents were ablaze! Leaping from warm sleeping bags, barefoot, we dashed to the adjacent lake and with pails of water succeeded in dousing the conflagration. Although our bare feet were lacerated from running over the sharp garnet crystals in the rock, we felt lucky — our sleeping tents were safe and safe too was the valuable data on our summer work. Even some food had been salvaged. We had lard, flour, sugar, salt and tea. Having no means to communicate our plight or request help, we existed on pancakes and tea until the supply plane arrived three weeks later. I've never liked pancakes since.

In the jungles, danger came from poisonous and disease-bearing insects. No one, neither myself nor my co-workers, escaped malaria for anti-malarial pills were not yet available. Animals were no danger, except if we surprised them — they had long ago learned to avoid men. But fish, with more primitive brains, still had to learn the same lesson and, in fact, flesh eaters like the piranha were a real danger to the unwary. Caution and common sense were our constant guides. Rarely were they forgotten and rarely did serious accidents and injuries occur.

A greater threat was other men. In Columbia at that time, nearly all adults outside the cities and large towns were armed — with a pistol if they were rich enough to afford one, otherwise with a knife. In the Llanos, men wore six-guns holstered on their hips and strutted like ragged little peacocks, often becoming involved in drunken senseless brawls with dire results. The primitive Indians of the region still used spears and poisoned arrows, and I remember well our one and only confrontation with them —

On a warm February evening in 1947, the North Americans on our crew had finished dinner and were sitting around the dining table, anticipating another monotonous night. The gas lanterns were lit and the radio was playing some popular South American music as large, winged insects flew around the light. Most of us were reading or writing letters or just daydreaming, when we heard the cry of "Fire!" from the nearby workers' camp.

Startled, we ran to check on what was happening, and discovered that about 800 feet from the camp the eight-foot high grass was burning and that the wind was swiftly driving the flames directly towards us. Then we noticed that new fires were springing to life along a distinct line. It was obvious that they were being purposely set and that someone was feeling quite unfriendly towards us. We quickly assessed the situation. We were under attack by wild Indians!

"Don't allow yourself to be silhouetted against the fire," we warned each other, realizing instinctively that hostile Indians would assume we'd run away from the fire, providing clear targets for other Indians, hidden in the darkness on the opposite side, to shoot at.

Our first worry was for our dynamite magazine where several tons of explosives were stored for use in our seismic explorations. Temporarily, it was safe (and therefore we were safe from it) as it was situated at least a quarter of a mile away at a far angle from the fire. Our next concern was for our camp and for our own immediate safety. The solution was simple — one of us leapt into a bulldozer and drove it straight towards the fire, scraping a fire-break in front of the camp. Within minutes the fire burned itself out.

The next morning we searched along the line where the fire had been set and, not surprisingly, found where the Indians, in panic, had abandoned their very crude bows and arrows and flint stones for making fire. In our imagination we visualized their consternation when, instead of destroying us, the fire aroused a roaring dragon with blazing yellow eyes which, with horrendous snorts and ghastly clanking, advanced upon them. Amused, we wondered how far and how long they had run. Although we searched, we found no traces of the other group of Indians who, we suspected, had been set to ambush us on the far side of the camp.

Personally, I felt an empathy for these primitive people whom we never saw. We were the invaders in their country. We were aliens, present without their permission, and, in a sense, they had the "right" of territorial possession to attack us.

Today, I understand that this area is now cultivated. Dams

have been erected, towns built, the land plowed and planted. I wonder if any of the shy native Indian population have survived? I wonder, too, how many people alive nowadays can claim to have been attacked by "Wild Indians"?

LOST

The Beaver, a one-engine bush plane, buzzed our temporary camp in Los Llanos, South America. After six weeks of gruelling work, I was due for a six-day leave with my wife in Bogota, the capital of Colombia, and I was excited and eager to be on my way. Gerry, the crew manager, had offered to drive me to our nearby "landing strip", a narrow swath of ground where our bulldozer had flattened the high grass. Just as we arrived, the plane, having hit the ground and taken a few high jumps, was finally taxiing to a stop.

"Hi, Squire," I greeted the pilot as he opened the door. After giving Gerry a goodbye handshake, I handed my map case to Squire and climbed aboard the tiny plane. I was the only passenger — not surprising, given the emptiness of that vast land — and taking my pick of the four seats available, I slung my small bag, containing toilet articles and a change of linen, into an overhead rack. After surviving the rough, bouncing take-off and with my stomach once again in its proper place, I relaxed to the drone of the small engine.

"Have another pickup to make before going on to Villavacencio," Squire informed me. I shrugged and swore under my breath — that meant waiting overnight before getting a plane to Bogota the next morning. Nothing to do about it, but sit back and relax. I pictured my wife and child and how good it would be to see them again and then wondered how early I could get a plane the next morning.

While looking at Squire's sure-handed

manipulations of the controls, I thought of what an unusual plane trip it was from Villavacencio to Bogota — more like an elevator ride than a flight. The distance between the two places was only about 50 miles, but Villavacencio, huddled at the base of the Andes Mountains, was only 700 feet above sea level while Bogota, on its elevated savannah, was another 8,300 feet higher up, with towering mountain peaks of 15,000 feet jutting up between the two locations. The plane had to corkscrew upwards 15,000 feet to clear those peaks, fly the few miles to Bogota, then corkscrew back down to its airport.

There was an alternative route through a pass, banned by the Ministry of Aviation, but often used nonetheless because it reduced the pilots' corkscrew climb to a mere 11,000 feet. It was a spectacular trip. At times the wings seemed ready to scrape the jagged naked rock of the canyon and the flowering bushes visible from the windows seemed close enough to touch. This was, of course, before jet planes, let alone the jumbo jets of today; at that time, the propeller driven DC 3 was the "state of the art."

Planes had sometimes crashed inside the pass, but only once did a near-catastrophe occur during one of my flights. In the middle of the pass, the most rugged spot, lay a right-angle turn, and the only way to navigate it was to steeply bank the plane. This particular time, I was watching the breathtaking scenery as we twisted along the pass when the engines suddenly went full throttle. The plane flipped upward and overhead baggage, papers and magazines flew through the air. Out of the window, as the plane performed an impossible manoeuvre, I caught a glimpse of the problem — the pass was fogged in around the corner! Somehow or other the pilot got the plane turned around within that constricted spot. We flew back and landed in Bogota. All the passengers were badly shaken. I waited for the pilot to disembark and asked,

"Th...th...that was a tight squeeze, wasn't it?"

White-faced, knees shaking, he replied, "Y...y...you're t...t...telling m...m...me?"

Chuckling to myself at the memory, I came back to my trip with Squire, focusing my eyes once more on his steady hands on the controls. After some time, I began to wonder where we were going since it was sure a long distance. More time passed and then Squire, looking back at me, ordered, "Hey, Bruce, come up here!"

I contorted my body to wedge into the co-pilot's seat. "I don't know where I am, Bruce," Squire informed me once I was in place. "We're lost." Then he giggled.

"You're kidding ... aren't you?" I could not believe he was serious.

"No, honestly!" he giggled again, but there was no humor in the giggle or in his sharp blue eyes. "I have no idea where we are."

"So let's go to town. Let's get to hell out of here."

"But I don't know where town is!"

"So, at least head west-north-west until we get to the mountains."

"But I don't know where north is either. I'm lost."

"So, look at your damn compass!"

"The compass is in town, getting repaired."

I looked at him in disbelief, as a sense of horror slowly began to come over me. He was serious. My God! We were lost somewhere over the upper reaches of the Amazon.

I stared at the ground below. The grassy plains had disappeared, replaced by moderately heavy jungle growth. And somewhere in that jungle were Indians who had an extraordinary art form — shrinking heads! Although it was illegal to sell these gruesome souvenirs, I had been approached to purchase them on several occasions previously — they were about the size of a large apple with long hair (the hair didn't shrink). The highest-priced head I was ever offered wore a magnificent red mustache and had obviously once been attached to the shoulders of some luckless European.

As I surveyed our situation, my first thought naturally enough, was "I must keep *my* head!"

I took a long look at Squire who had placed us in such a dire predicament — a handsome, boyish looking Englishman, 6 feet 2 inches tall, with blond hair and penetrating blue eyes. What did I know about him? He owned an 'airline', consisting of a total of two small bush planes and he had been a fighter pilot in the Battle of Britain. In that battle he completed three tours of duty and was three time the sole survivor of the various squadrons to which he was assigned. I could just imagine him scrambling in his Spitfire, rising to meet the invading German Air Aramada and giggling his nervousness as he attacked.

After volunteering for a fourth tour of duty, the British Air Ministry became aware of his record, declared him a hero, gave him a bunch of medals, and sent him to Canada to exhort the colonists to increase their support of the war. Discovering he preferred drinking to making speeches, he was then given an honorary position in India where he spent the rest of the war. To him, flying without a compass would be a small risk, virtually negligible in comparison to the desperate fighting he'd done.

"Got any ideas what we should do?" he asked without much hope.

Finding directions was the first priority. Where was the sun? That would determine west since it was past mid-afternoon by then. Looking upwards, I observed that a thick bank of clouds was shading the sun and surmised that the plane was too underpowered to climb above those clouds. Squire agreed in a despondent tone of voice that my conclusion was probably right and that we had better conserve our fuel.

"Take the plane down, just over the trees, and when we reach a river, follow it," I ordered.

In a few minutes, we saw a good-sized river. We agreed on the direction it was flowing and, since rivers in that area generally flow eastward, away from the mountains, a direction was established.

"Fly north and let's confirm our direction with another river," I suggested. This done, we set our course for the Andes. One and a half hours later, the mountains appeared on the horizon. I estimated that nightfall was no more than an hour away.

"Okay, Squire," I said, "Now which way? Right or left to Villavacencio? And, incidentally, how much gas is left?"

"We've got just enough for about another hour's flying. It'll be dark by then , so we'll have to land soon — and I still don't know where in hell town. I just don't know which way to go from here," he said, adding his humorless giggle.

"You must have some idea......some way to guess," I insisted.

"Honestly, Bruce, I don't. I got us into this mess. Sorry. It's your life, so you guess."

Taking a deep breath, I decided, "Turn left."

The fact that I'm now writing this story confirms that I guessed correctly. In 45 minutes the lights of the village of Villavacencio came shining through the gathering dusk. I have a somewhat hazy, blurred recollection that we drank an awful lot of rum that night.

The lesson learned? — relying on simple common sense, that most uncommon of talents, is usually the most effective way to handle problems. It got us more than halfway home. Luck or intuition was the last resort.

Chapter 12

Nasturtium

"How's your Dad doing, Robert? I hear from your Mom fairly often and she just says he's fine when I ask. But I sense she's concerned about him."

"Yeah, Mom worries about him alright. Nothing specific, at least as far as I know. Of course, they're both getting older. Next birthday, Dad will be 48. That was the same age you were when you retired, wasn't it? Mom worries about how hard he works. I think he's doing okay financially but he hardly ever takes a break. He wants to make a lot more money and isn't very happy. Sometimes they argue. She tells him to slow down but he shouts that she just doesn't understand and claims he's never going to stop. I think she worries he'll get a heart attack or something. How come you retired so early, Papa? Was there some reason you had to? Did you ever regret it?"

"My decision to retire is an example of how the material and inspirational can integrate, how mystery and practical reasoning can combine. I remember well that day I decided . . .

A crystal-clear morning. Nature held its breath, fearful of breaking the spell of its own perfection. During the night a rumor of the coming winter had whispered through the mountains leaving the season's first white dusting of snow on the peaks of Mount Rundle high above me. The strike and dip of its massive slabs of limestone were etched into sharp relief against the sky's pure blue. Below, the dark pine-treed valley wore bright yellow splashes of tamarack, aspen and poplar while misty silver ghosts sedately rose from the Bow River.

I was attending an international geophysical conference at the Banff Springs Hotel. The first morning, I knew, would be devoted to the ritual intoning of monotonous welcoming speeches. I had no intention of attending *that*. The morning was mine, for myself alone.

Leaving the hotel, I slowly strolled along the forest trails that skirted the river to the Cascades of Time — that summer garden with its many little waterfalls. That late fall morning, however, no water flowed. All was silent. Perhaps time too had stopped. Sitting down on a low stone wall which bordered a large bed of orange nasturtiums which shone brightly in the magnified air, I plucked one of the round, Roman shield-shaped leafs. I chewed it slowly, savoring its fresh peppery flavor. Reminiscing, I recalled when, as a child, I first ate one and thought I was the first person in the world to make a wonderful new discovery. I remembered too the childhood guilt for having stolen the leaf from a neighbor's garden.

I welcomed this time to myself for I needed a quiet time to just think, to order my thoughts, to decide where I was going. An important decision lay ahead — a crossroad on my life's journey — a place where other avenues diverged from the path I presently travelled.

I reviewed how, six years previously, I had severed an unfortunate business association and started afresh — how with a mere $60,000, the total extent of my fortune, I resolved to found an independent oil company — and how, fortunately, the first three wells drilled were all successful. I recalled the sequence of rapid growth after that — investors buying shares — the drilling of more and more wells (not all successfully) — the acquiring of more and more assets — the expansion into foreign countries — the ever-increasing income and profit. But the company too was nearing a crossroads where changes would be needed.

At that time, only my secretary and myself work for the company, although consultants were hired as needed. Now the company had grown too big to be operated like that much longer. To continue to expand, a large staff consisting of geologists, engineers, geophysicists, accountants, draughtpersons, secretaries and so on would be needed. At this juncture in the company's affairs such an expansion was the natural, normal, expected course for it to follow.

On the other hand, did I personally want to follow that path? Would not all my time be devoted to boring corporate matters and to supervising others instead of having the excitement of doing it myself — formulating concepts where oil and gas might be trapped, conducting the exploration, raising the money for drilling, supervising the drilling itself, and having the personal triumph of success? That is what I had done, but having done it, I asked myself, what challenge remained? There appeared to be little opportunity for anything new and little fun in repeating something again and again. Had I not accomplished all I had set out to do both professionally and financially? To acquire more and more for the sake of more and more seemed a senseless goal.

Of course another avenue to follow was not to expand the company, not hire staff, continue the status quo and rest on my laurels. I could draw a fine salary, manage its routine affairs, attempt no new projects, and let the company stagnate. I smiled to myself for I knew the impossibility of following that route. I knew myself. Not only would I feel I was being unfair to the other shareholders, but I knew I could not sit still. I had too much energy, too many fresh ideas, too much desire to always venture further. No, that path held no attraction whatsoever.

These were the only routes available for the company to follow and only the first, expanding and growing, was really satisfactory. And, in fact, this was the path that eventually it did follow for many years.

Yet one more path beckoned me — a path for myself alone. That trail was indistinct, overgrown with weeds and brambles, for few had passed that way. It was the path that had been taken by prophets, sages, and great teachers. It was the path that led through a wilderness - a desert place - a mountain cave - a deep forest - some secret retreat where one faced oneself alone. Where the path led beyond there, I could not guess. A mistiness hid its destination. To travel the length of that path, I knew I would have to be free of all encumbrances. To follow that path I would have to sell my company and let someone else be its guide.

Instinctively I drew back from such a strange course of action. Life was good in all respects — wife, children, home, health, friends, and now, for the first time, financial stability. Who in their right mind would want to disturb such an enviable idyllic state of affairs? Why would I wish to leave the safety, security and comfort of the known for a path whose end was unsure, unknown? Who would have such courage?

On the other hand, I remembered the goals I had set myself almost a quarter of a century previously in South America. All had been achieved but one. Remaining was my goal to retire at 48 with all the money I wanted and then to devote time and energy to my spiritual journey. That goal could now be reached.

Of course that spiritual path was not entirely unexplored. I had travelled it some considerable distance and many of the experiences I've described in these pages had already occurred but much, much more remained. I had always known that someday I would pursue that path to its farthest destination for, once started, it can never be abandoned. A still voice had always whispered, calling to me, enticing me to follow. It was the way home. But I did not guess that someday could be today.

How many stages are there in Man's life, I mused? Obviously, the time spent from birth to adulthood constitutes the first stage — a growing stage — a time of learning — a time to discover how to walk, talk, feed and care for ourselves — a time of learning the skills of a chosen trade or profession — a time to become familiar with this world in which we find ourselves.

Just as obvious, there is a second stage — a time to apply our skills, employ our trade or profession, earn a living — a time to contribute to the common wealth, the well-being of our tribe, community or nation — and a time for family, a precious time to love and, in turn, to instruct our young in what life skills we were taught or discovered and found useful.

The third stage is much less obvious. In Western culture, at least until recently, Man has been expected to continue working in the second stage until as old age approaches and life's energy diminishes, he is retired to a final stage where he "reaps his reward." Too tired and too late to venture far afield, most cling to their accustomed places and do the things they always did. Their "reward" too often is a hollow promise, an empty illusion.

How cultures differ. In ancient China, the third stage was no time for rest and retirement. It was the most vital part of life. For this stage, they believed, Man was created. As soon as possible, the earlier in life the better, as soon as one's commitments to family and community were fulfilled, Man was expected to venture into the third stage — the search for wisdom.

Hindus agreed that this three-stage progression constituted a proper life but added a fourth, a most important stage. If wisdom was found and spiritual enlightenment achieved, then such wise ones were expected to complete their life cycle by devoting the rest of their days to sharing, teaching and imparting that rare wisdom to others. With further consideration I decided these four stages were not exclusive stages, for obviously we learn during all of our life and, using what we learn, teach others by example.

The quandary I faced was whether to make the spiritual path the exclusive focus in my life for I knew to arrive at its destination that all my time, all my strength, all my heart, and all my mind would be required. Now I had time. Now I had health and vigor. Now I had sufficient wealth to provide for my needs. Now I was at the height of my mental ability. Yet what grave doubts assailed me!

If I sold my company and abandoned my career and profession, who would understand? Would I not be considered a fool to give up what I had worked so hard to achieve? How many friends would walk away from me? Would I have enough money? What if I lost it or inflation eroded it away? What if I was broke after I passed a point of no return, when my business and professional expertise had grown obsolete? Then what if the path led nowhere? What if I became lost and was doomed like a nomad to wander forever trying to find what I was not quite sure existed? I did not want to be alone, feeling deserted and abandoned. What if ——? What if ——?

At this point in my musing, I was not attempting to arrive at a final decision on my future. I was, however, very precisely defining the problem, envisioning and mentally listing all the possible options. Problems, I had learned, could only be solved when the problem was clearly and explicitly defined and all possible solutions itemized. There was certainly no urgency in arriving at a decision for, in any event, I wanted to satisfactorily complete the exploration and drilling program in which my company was currently engaged. A year at least would pass before that was accomplished. There was no rush. My decision could wait. Surprisingly, however, the answer came both swiftly and dramatically.

Suddenly the silence was shattered, my train of thought interrupted. An enormous bumble bee had arrived to frantically collect the last of summer's nectar from the nasturtiums. Fascinated, I watched as the bumble bee in a buzzing fervor flew from flower to flower. The striations on the petals pointed the way below stamen and pistil to where the flower's long spur was filled full with the desired nectar. There were brief intervals of silence as the bee consumed the sweet drops of each yielding flower.

Joining the bee in its feast, I idly plucked and ate another nasturtium leaf. What did I know about nasturtiums? Oh, yes — Nasturtiums belonged to the cress family and its leaves, containing ten times more vitamin C than lettuce, shared the fresh peppery taste of its more commonly consumed cousins, peppercress and watercress. The petals too were edible and could lend a touch of the exotic to salads, contributing both their color and their pungent taste. The seeds too, when pickled, made a fine peppery relish to accompany meats. Linnaeus, the great botanist, who in 1752 originally formulated the classification of plants still used today, made a most curious claim about nasturtiums. He stated that his daughter, Elizabeth Christina, had observed the flowers to spontaneously emit electric sparks. Although this is discredited by modern botanists (who may never have really looked), the phenomenon has also been reported by others, including no less a genius and observer of life than Goethe himself.

The sun was warming the day. It felt good on my back. I was still, at peace, my attention gently resting on one particular bloom, half lost in its beauty and perfection. Did the flower enrapture the bee as it did me? Suddenly I felt as if I was being drawn towards it, as if it was a magnet too strong to resist. I sensed I was falling, falling into that one flower. I seemed somehow to become smaller and smaller until I was within its five-petalled corona. Shining through the orange petals, the light created an orange world whose orange perimeters appeared to recede further and further the smaller I grew. I sank deeper, floating downwards, into the spur of the flower, then deeper yet into oblivion, into nothingness. I disappeared entirely. While physically I existed no longer, beyond the physical, beyond and beyond the beyond, my spirit was liberated. Here neither doubts nor fears remained. All was glory and ecstasy. The answers to the cosmic riddles were almost in my grasp.

I know not what time passed until I returned to myself. Perhaps no time at all had elapsed in the world. It seemed the same bee buzzed on its way to invade the next flower. But something had changed. My future, the path I would take had been determined. Mine would be the less travelled trail.

That evening during a reception and cocktail party at the hotel, I casually mentioned to three or four that my company might be for sale. Rumor, I knew, would do the rest. One year later, all my commitments to investors and partners satisfied, I sold all my assets and retired from business and my professional career. I was free — free to follow my ecstasy!

Chapter 13
Beyond the End of Time

"When Half-Gods Go, Then God Appears"

Early evening and the promise of a great sunset. We walk the short distance to the beach and find a large log to sit on, the waves lapping the rocks near our feet. The city din fades, seems far away. The seagulls' screams hush with the ending of the day.

My mind drifts — Mom — Dad — home — what am I going to do? — a job? — university? — got to make up my mind — and my new girlfriend, what about her? — and only four days left before I have to leave — don't feel like going — at least I learnt a lot from Papa — I seem to be out of questions — guess I've learned all I can from him.

Each lost in our thoughts, we watch the sun sink below the ocean's horizon. Time passes, the silence an intimate communion. The colors in the heavens deepen, then slowly fade. Still we sit. Dusk grows closer, the first stars now apparent, the city behind us a fairyland of lights.

Musingly, softly, almost to himself, Papa begins to speak . . .

Today, how rare it is to really see the sky at night — to see into the depths of the galaxy, to see the Milky Way glow, to see shooting stars abruptly flash and burn and man-made satellites speed between the multi-colored stars. How far we must retreat into the shrinking wilderness to escape the lights of civilization, which obscure the lights of heaven. Yet on these rare occasions, lying on our backs and gazing endlessly, what sights we see, such imaginings we have, what dreams we dream. A feeling of reverent awe overwhelming us, we become enchanted, entrapped in wonderment. How insignificant is man against that greatness! How splendid the mysteries! We wonder: How did it all begin? How will it end? Who or what created it? And for what reason? What does it all mean? And what are we in that vast scheme?

We ache, long wistfully to know, to uncover the hidden threads to unravel the riddles of the universe, to whisper the secret charm to shatter the spell and unveil those mysteries. Somehow we feel that a profound revelation lies just beyond our grasp.

Many and varied are the myths, legends and beliefs told of creation ranging from simplistic tales to profound insights. Some verge on the humorous, for instance, the creation story of the primitive northern hill tribes in Thailand:

> God became pregnant (whodunit was not explained!). With excitement and curiosity as to what the offspring might be, She waited impatiently for millennia to pass. Finally She gave birth. But what She gave birth to was — a pumpkin!
>
> In fury and disgust at such a paltry result from Her long labour, She hurled the poor pumpkin at a mountain where, with a loud Plop!, it burst. The good sticky seeds adhered to the mountain sides while the poorer, drier seeds fell to the valley below. The seeds were transformed into Man with the hill people, originating from the best seeds, being naturally superior to all the people below.

India, where the religions of both Buddhism and Hinduism originated, has been fascinated by the mysteries of creation since time immemorial. Finding the truth through spiritual insights is considered to be the proper task of each individual. While India has no written histories because Hindus consider nothing of any real importance has occurred since the time that Krishna lived, the spiritual aspirant has available rich traditions and a wealth of books and scrolls to assist him. Of these, the most ancient and revered teachings are contained in the Rig Veda (Veda means knowledge). The origin of the Rig Veda is believed to date back 15,000 years, long before writing was invented.

Pundits are men who have memorized and chant the various Vedas, Shrutis, and Smirtis that comprise their ancient teachings. From earliest times, these Pundits have taught their sons to memorize the verses of wisdom word for word and so the knowledge has passed from generation to generation for these thousands of years. When writing was first invented ten thousand years after the first recitation of the Rig Veda, it and the other great Hindu literary works were inscribed. What the Pundits chant in India today is identical, word for word, to the earliest manuscripts still in existence and presumably is also word-perfect from the first time it was uttered so many thousands of years before that. Thus the purity of the original teaching has been maintained.

Once I had the opportunity to hear a Pundit chanting the Rig Veda while, after each verse, an English translation was made. Immediately my scalp began to tingle and I experienced 'deja vu' as I listened to its vision of creation. That vision of the beginning, preservation and the final ending of the Universe was identical to a vision I too had had! It explained the mystery of the Cosmos — how and why it was created, and how it will all end.

I had never spoken of my vision or revelation prior to hearing the Rig Veda for I'd had no words to convey its dimensions and splendor. Now, with the ancient concepts of the cosmology of the Hindus and the current concepts of the cosmos of the Astro-physicists, I have, at last, a vocabulary to attempt it. First, let me define that vocabulary.

- **Brahma** - is God expressing as the Creator. Brahma is the Originator of all that is, has been and ever will be.
- **Vishnu** - is God expressing as the Savior, Sustainer, Preserver and Supporter of the universe and all it contains.
- **Shiva** - is God expressing as the Destroyer, the Annihilator, and Finality. Shiva is the end to which not only life but Creation itself returns. Shiva dances to the rhythm of the universes and laughs at the Cosmic Joke. Of the Trinity, Shiva

is the Deity most commonly prayed to because the supplicant prays that Shiva will destroy his ignorance.

These three Gods personify the natural forces continuously at play throughout the Cosmos.

- **Brahman** - is God beyond expressing. Brahman is the Supreme, the One God, the All, the Great Spirit. While the three Deities described above are manifestations of Brahman, Brahman is beyond all that is and all that is not.
- **Prime Ylium** - is the universe at the very instant of its creation, the "Big Bang" of physicists. Infinitesimally small with infinite energy, it explodes out of the void, the silence, the no-thing-ness, producing the time, space, energies, and matter which compose our physical universe.
- **Black Holes** - are the end products from the death of stars that are more than four times the size of our sun. As they collapse internally, their matter is so tightly squeezed together that it is literally squeezed out of existence. Its gravity is so enormous that even light cannot escape its hold. As it whips through its orbit in space, everything that comes near its gravity grasp, is sucked into oblivion.
- **White Holes** - Much credence is given by astrophysicists to the theory that our entire universe will ultimately collapse into one final black hole. Perhaps, some believe, such a black hole becomes a White Hole, the Prime Ylium of another universe and thus the Cosmos continuously oscillates between nothingness and existence.
- **Multiple Universes** - an infinite number of other universes may co-exist with ours. The Quantum Theory allows for this possibility.

The Vision

One evening I was in my den, surrounded by my books, listening to a Mahler symphony. As the music ceased, I floated into a peaceful silence, idly daydreaming. I drifted on this gentle stream of reverie but briefly for the current rapidly quickened. In a rush I felt as if I was swept over a waterfall, across a precipice of reality and plunged into the depths of my being, to a dark, silent and incredibly peaceful place. Slowly the contents of my den seemed to melt — the desk, the chair, the lounge on which I had been sitting, the books and the bookcase, the pictures on the wall — and then to flow, to stream away, until, rushing ever faster, they too were swept over the precipice to be absorbed into the depths. Then the entire house melted and flowed and was drawn to the abyss. Even more quickly the yard outside, the neighbor's houses, the street itself started to flow. Faster and faster the process continued, the district where I lived, the whole city, the entire province in turn poured into a flooding, roaring river and over the edge of existence. Swelling in even greater floods that strange river raced until the entire nation, the North American continent, the whole world itself flowed and fell into a silent and peaceful depth. It dawned on me that somehow *I* was that unfathomable depth, that silence! I became that which absorbed all things. I was Shiva! A black hole!

Swelling with a love towards all things, all things were irresistibly pulled into my orbit, my aura. There, separation ceased and all became a unity. I called the ten thousand trillion things home. Expanding with love, I became an enormous vortex spinning in space, an incredible whirlpool of blackness and emptiness, sucking into my peaceful dark depths the entire solar system. Faster still I spun, ever increasing the magnetic fatal attraction. The nearer stars now flowed towards me and were absorbed, their lights extinguished. Now the farther stars rushed in a cosmic maelstrom towards me and were absorbed as well, ceasing to be. Ever tighter I held them, squeezed in my passionate embrace until light, energy and matter ceased to exist separately, unable to resist the enormous gravity-pull of love. I was the quieting of all turmoil, the cessation of all struggle and movement, oblivion, the consummation of peace.

Of our galaxy of hundreds of thousands of millions of stars nothing was left, everything was extinguished and silenced. Now the hundreds of thousands of millions of other galaxies, whirling, wheeling and twisting at ever greater speeds, gravitated, swirling into my yawning vortex, my well of irrisistible love, until not only the entire universe but time and space itself ended. Ultimately, there was nothing—no-thing at all. Without dimensions I was a point, a singularity. The final black hole! I was Shiva in eternal sleep. Eternal night.

I cannot judge how many minutes went by in my den nor what timeless eons passed where I existed. Nor does it matter. The next thing I knew I was startled by a sharp, loud sound—a clear pure note unlike anything ever imagined. High pitched, like a mighty gale screaming through high-tension transmission wires, it contained all the vowels of creation.

Silence had been shattered, nothingness obliterated; I was Shiva no longer. Where had the sound originated? I searched for its source and became that source. Now I was Brahma, the Creator, my trumpet heralding the dawn of Genesis.

I, Brahma, was pure love and forced by joy, by ecstasy, to express that love, the sole essence of my being. Out of nothingness love burst the bounds of the Void in one majestic note, the Prime Ylium, the 'Big Bang' of the universe. My glorious song of pent-up passion; the creative energy of the cosmos. That first note reverberated against the nothingness and echoed back upon itself forming harmonics. Again and again the golden note reverberated while the harmonies increased until the first chord was produced. With ever increasing complexities, the chords became primal energy, which, echoing and re-echoing and reverberating ever stronger and stronger, became light. Time and space were invented. Out of the fire mist, morning was born. It was the springtime of the universe!

Whirlwinds of energies intertwined, wove latticeworks which patterned matter. Patterns dissolved back into chaos, became light and whorls of energy once more, then reformed, producing more complicated lattices of matter. Raw matter coalesced into enormous clouds of dust which fused and jelled into hundreds of thousands of millions of galaxies with gigantic suns. These multitudes of suns, vast, extravagant balls of heat and light, exploded in turn, to bond and congeal into thousands of lesser suns.

The original note became fainter, obscured by the ever increasing loudness of the chaotic expansion of creation. I had been Brahma. I had sung my song of love until creation, in all its complexity, became a symphony. I now became that fuller sound, the harmonic melody of that symphony, its essence reverberating as my essence. I became Vishnu, the Preserver, the Saviour, the Sustainer of life, the Keeper of being, existence itself. The Universe changed ceaselessly, expanded, paused, changed and expanded again. I gloried while the Universe unfolded into splendor after splendor of pulsating wholeness. I saw the galaxies slowly rotating; suns swinging in the arms of far-flung island universes with some of the suns, in turn, swinging multi-colored planets around themselves. A few of these planets vibrated with life and consciousness. All was good, perfect. The cosmos throbbed with love. It had always been so, for I, Vishnu, was eternal.

Then, after eons of time, even deeper into my being I went. I now seemed to be apart, at a distance, in awe and wonder at the magnificence of the cosmos, infinity and eternity. I had become an observer, a witness, no longer participating, no longer involved, no longer

Shiva, Brahma or Vishnu. From my new vantage point I observed all three Deities, the great primal forces of nature co-existing, all acting simultaneously, for they operated in an eternity where time and sequence did not exist. Brahma everlastingly created — there was an infinite number of universes; Vishnu forever preserved them and Shiva continuously destroyed.

I felt the pulse, the heartbeat of our cosmos; that pulse whose present beat began 15 billion years ago and will not cease until another 20 billion years pass; that pulse which will pause until the next beat throbs a universe forth once more.

Long after the vision ended, and indeed for many years, I was puzzled. Never did I doubt its reality. But where had I been to see such things? And what, I wondered, am I to have received such a revelation? What am I to have seen what a great seer had once before experienced and described in the Rig Veda?

Scientists and philosophers using observation and logic have pondered the mysteries of the universe throughout history, but the ultimate knowledge of reality is not gleaned in that manner. Being it, experiencing it, far beyond all scientific or philosophical methods, means to know it in our deep inner core. Like that ancient seer, I too, had been a see-er. I had been it and experienced it. I had been the actors, the Deities, in the drama of the cosmos.

What exactly is a revelation? It is not a dream or nightmare which are stress release mechanisms and rooted in real life experiences, however distorted. It is not a hallucination brought on by drugs or illness. A revelation or vision has these characteristics:

. It may occur while either waking or sleeping.

. It is beyond ordinary imagining, beyond our common understanding, beyond ancestral memories. I've used words like feeling and seeing to describe it because I know no others, but it is far beyond our physical senses. It is quite indescribable. Words can only hint at the actuality.

. The recipient, the see-er, feels a sacred gift has been granted from a holy, higher realm.

. The validity is beyond doubt, never questioned by the see-er.

. It is repeatable, just as my vision was the same as the vision of the unknown see-er of the Rig Veda, 15,000 years previously.

Sometimes, months or even years after I experience a great insight or revelation, the vision is further extended and intensified, its further totality disclosed. It's as if the Teacher knew my limitation of understanding and wished not to reveal other chapters or teach other lessons until I was ready. Such was the case with this vision.

Ten years passed. During that time I'd heard the complete Rig Veda translated, although some of its passages remained obscure to me. Now, however, I was about to understand them for my revelation was about to expand and clarify. And once again it was to be identical with the vision of the original see-er of that ancient text.

At this time I was on a six-week meditation retreat in a small village in upper New York state. One warm, sunny, early spring day, while strolling along a country road, I came upon a large paved rectangle. Obviously, it had formerly been the floor of a very large building but I could not imagine what sort of building it had been nor, in that remote area, what purpose it could have served. As I walked across the paving I noticed how the cement had been cracked and broken into large slabs which had been heaved asunder by winter frost and vegetation. I stopped and stared at the soft grasses and delicate pink flowers growing in the cracks. Pensive, I mused how life, seemingly so uncertain and fragile, was actually powerful, persistent and sufficiently irresistible to burst through the cement.

My mind wandered freely over such thoughts and conjectures while I stared at one perfect little pink flower.

Without warning, my mind frame shifted. Once more the whole vision I had previously experienced was repeated. Again in quick succession I actually experienced being Shiva, Brahma and Vishnu. I realized how each expressed love, were love, for Brahma created from love, Vishnu preserved with love and Shiva called all loves home once more. Then, as before, I seemed to stand apart, to be a witness, a mere observer, uninvolved with the turbulence of the cosmos. I enjoyed the view, the drama of the Trinity of Deities at continuous play, the Black and White Holes, the multiplicities of universes each with their billions of stars. Once more I heard the rhythm. Once more I saw the dance. But again, I saw it as if I were at a distance from it. I, myself, was beyond time, sequences or successions, beyond where everlasting change occurred.

"What am I, to have such a vision?" I wondered again. "And, even more strange, where am I now, to be existing apart from and witnessing all of creation as if it were below me or over there?"

Then I began to sense an awesome Presence, a Presence not only beyond change and beyond time and space but beyond the cosmos itself. It enveloped all creation, expressed itself as the Trinity of Deities, but was not contained or limited or circumscribed by them or by any thing. Words and phrases flashed through my mind: unmoving and unmovable, ever present, all knowing, all powerful, the One God, non-attached, beyond comprehension, indescribable, the THAT, I AM!

Brahman! I sensed Its eternal silence, Its awesome power. Trembling, I touched It. I felt It. I knew It. It absorbed me, like a sponge absorbs water. Instilled, I became It.

I cannot describe the Bliss, the Ecstasy. I saw the

cosmos from Brahman's unique perspective. I was literally where Brahman is. And I understood that if I was where Brahman is, then I am Brahman and you are Brahman and all is Brahman. Beyond the end of time itself, as One Spirit, we are, have ever been, infinite and eternal. Oneness. Unity.

Slowly and reluctantly, the vision faded. Surprised, I found I was just myself once more, still standing on broken stone, staring at one little, pink flower.

Chapter 14
Separation and Return

The smell of coffee and sizzling bacon. I am preparing our breakfast which includes a specialty of New Mexico — scrambled eggs laced with various hot peppers and cheeses.

Afterwards, as we enjoy our second cup of coffee, he asks me if I remember our hikes to Jackpine Point. Not only do I remember them well, but I want to go there again. It's a perfect day for it. After tidying the apartment, we drive to our destination, Lighthouse Park.

I lead the way into the shaded forest. Only the gentlest of breezes trickle through the lush vegetation although a strong wind bends the tree tops 200 feet above. The only other sound on the crude trail is the falling of the occasional loose rock dislodged by our passing until I become aware that Papa is breathing hard. He is having difficulty keeping up for my pace has been brisk and steady, whether the path led up or down. I stop deep in the forest and say, "Hey Papa, I remember you teaching me the names of the trees. Bet I still remember — these tall ones with even bark and flat needle are hemlocks, over there are the lacy branched cedars, these moss-covered ones with foot-wide leaves are maples and over there with red, peeling bark is an arbutus and this huge one is a Douglas fir whose crushed needles smell like orange peel."

We both crush and smell the needles before I continue, "I remember a lot of things you used to tell me. I remember you told me the beliefs that Indians have about trees; that trees are living creatures who, like themselves, belong to the land; that trees have a distinct personality like men — some are friendly, others unfriendly and when injured or cut, they hurt and bleed like we do; and that trees move around, but very slowly and that they breathe, but only once a day; and that a tree's sense of time differs from Man's, for many were mature centuries before the first white man appeared; and finally they believe that trees are aware, conscious beings who barely discern men, little panting creatures who momentarily flit about at their base, then disappear. They wonder what we are and what our hurry is."

"Right, Robert, and do you remember me showing you how Indians walk silently through the forest; how they glide, their toes touching the ground before the heel? Like this?" he asks, illustrating. I didn't tell him I'd forgotten.

"The Indians in the Southwest don't walk that way," I inform him, "but they're desert, not forest people. Now I remember—didn't you say that when we walked that way, our feet automatically sense a secure platform with no stumbling over roots or tripping on stones? Let's do it again. You go first."

Following his lead, gliding silently, we become part of the forest. Often we pause, our heads slightly tilted, expectant, listening. We hear the forest messages. Sniffing the air, we read its humid scent. Now and then we cup a wild flower to peer into its depth. Now we stroke the soft warm bark of a tree over 30 feet in circumference. Now we listen to the singing of a miniature waterfall. Now we caress a leaf. No longer do we intrude upon the forest. We are with friends.

Jackpine Point, I rediscover on arrival, is a sheer granite promontory high above the sea. Below, the huge Pacific swells smash against the rock and, furious at having their passage blocked, send white torrents clawing up the cliff. Stunted Jackpines, whose thick trunks betray their age, are wind twisted into surrealistic shapes. At the cliff edge I fling my arms wide and, laughing, I lean against the sea-sprayed gale.

Then, finding a flat bench of rock out of the wind, we sit together enjoying the scene—islands, boats, mountains. Papa says he needs the rest.

We sit quiet, absorbing the atmosphere until, rather wistfully, I state, "You have experienced so much, you know so much."

"It's a paradox. We can't know anything until we know everything."

"I'm not sure I quite understand —."

"A part only makes sense in relation to the whole. We will only know ourselves and our world when we grasp the interrelatedness of everything, the unity, the all-ness. Only then can we fully appreciate and understand uniqueness," he explains.

"And do you know everything?" I wonder.

"I have experienced unity but that does not mean I understand all things or that I possess all skills and specialized techniques. If you have a headache, don't let me operate. I'm no brain surgeon," he chuckles.

I grin and then become thoughtful once more. How stupid I'd been yesterday to think I had learnt all I could from Papa. I've barely touched the surface of his depths. Have I wasted my visit by asking him about unimportant things? And how can I frame proper questions now?

"I want to ask you so much, yet I'm not sure what to ask. At university a group of us used to get together and talk about philosophical things. Perhaps I can't do better than to start by asking you questions like one of the questions propounded by the Greeks 2500 years ago: `From whence do we come?' Or if we're all one Spirit as you experienced 'Beyond the End of Time', why don't we know it? Why do we feel we're separate individuals? And, more importantly, is there some way to really know what we are?"

He remains silent for some time, staring out to sea. Finally he replies. . .

When I experienced Brahma, the Creator, I experienced It as a point source, an immense intensity of pure sublime love. That love demanded expression. Its expression was creation.

One of the statements all religions agree on is, "In the beginning there was God." Not God and something else. So when God created, He/She created from Her/Himself—for nothing else existed. God said, "Let there be light"—and there was light. Light is God expressing—not from a heavenly factory or warehouse but from His/Herself. All of creation, the whole cosmos, is the expression and manifestation of that Love that the Creator is.

To better understand this thought, consider the analogy of the ocean and ocean waves. Just as waves do not exist separate and apart from the ocean, so you and I and all the trillion, trillion components of creation are not separate or apart from God. If we dip a bucket into the waves, we get a bucket of ocean water, not a bucket of waves. A wave is simply an individuation of the ocean, just as all things in the world are individuations of the Creator. As the ocean expresses itself in the form of waves, so the Creator expresses His love as light and galaxies and stars and planets and ocean and land and forests and animals and you and me. 'From whence do we come?' We come from God.

Now, if we are expressions of God, why do we all see ourselves as distinct, separate individuals and not in Unity with the Creator? Let's explore that question in depth . . . After our conception, all our primary needs for food and warmth are satisfied within our mother's womb. We are one with mother and have no sense of ourselves as separate beings. We are in Unity. Things change immediately after birth, however, as soon as we experience the common sensations of cold, wet and hunger, and too soon learn that our needs are not instantaneously satisfied. We sense a growing separation—we are separate and distinct from mother, with wants that are often quite different from hers. We experiment and soon discover how to get what we want—and Ego, the self, is born. If we cry loudly and express anger or hurt, our needs are met sooner. Mother no longer holds us all the time, but if we cry or demonstrate happiness and smile and gurgle, she tends to hold us longer. Our sense of self or Ego continues to grow and we compete with the surrounding environment to get what we want. Ego is not a negative attribute for without ego, we would not survive. Ego demands that our wants and needs be filled.

As we grow through experience, our emotions become crystallized and we have thoughts and feelings about them. The sensation of hunger, for example, becomes "I feel hungry" or "I am hungry." Gradually, we begin to arrive at simple judgements such as "I don't like being hungry," and to discriminate between experiences, arriving at even more complex judgments such as "Mother gives me food and attention more often than Father." We form opinions like "Mother is nicer than sister and sister is nicer than brother." By this time—the end of our first year—our individuation is complete and our ego well established. Then we enter the next stage of our growth, that of the "terrible twos," when we establish and strengthen the boundary between our ego and the rest of the world.

We form an infinite number of opinions as we grow older and these, with the help of family and peers, coalesce into belief systems—"we are better than them," for example; or "we know the truth while all those catholics, unitarians, democrats, communists or whatever are wrong, evil or stupid, etc." We assume modes of behavior, join gangs, form groups, adhere to the mores and second-hand rules of our particular society, find our place within it and believe that we are different from other groups. In the final stage of individuation, we assume the roles we will play throughout our lives, identifying with our position in the family—"I am a brother, mother, sister, etc."; with our chosen profession—"I am a lawyer, prostitute, steelworker, etc."; and with our habits—"I am a big eater, a jogger, a social drinker, etc." We each play a large number of roles and are each the writer, producer and star of our own unique melodrama entitled, "My Life."

By the time we reach adulthood, we've grown far away from the spiritual essence of our being. We are so involved with living and solving our problems, how could we *not* have forgotten our origins, what we truly are? Naturally, we see ourselves as unique and separate beings.

After birth, like a new wave on the ocean, we recognize other waves of varying sizes around us. As we grow, the larger waves diminish and fade away and new waves are born. Constantly we see change, impermanence. Eventually we, too, become a big wave and then, gradually, we also begin to fade. We sense our individuality, our solitary existence separate from all other waves, having long ago forgotten our universal source and the fact that we are all manifestations of the same ocean, and we consider the question, "From whence do we come?" to be a great mystery.

Ocean waves provide an useful analogy for understanding other matters as well. For instance, of the infinite number of waves on the ocean, one rarely stands out much more than the rest. But once in a long, long time, the rhythm of the waves is such that several waves come into phase so that a giant wave is formed and towers 100 feet or more above all the rest. While its life may be short, it has great significance. There are rare cases where a ship's radio has been in routine contact with shore when such a giant wave has struck. The day may be pleasant, the seas tranquil with no hint of impending danger. Then all contact is lost as the ship is swamped, torn to pieces and instantly thrust into the depths without a trace.

Unlike waves, you and I have free will. We can choose our dimensions, our importance, our significance, during our brief appearance on earth. Most lives are insignificant and remain insignificant until one makes the decision to become significant. Thus, throughout history a few individuals tower above all the rest. They are the giant waves of destiny. They are the movers and shakers of the world. They have chosen to make a difference, to be significant. You and I also have that choice.

Now let's go deeper. How can we recognize what we really are? We have looked at how the ego develops and realize that we could not survive without it. But we see, too, how the ego has given us a sense of separateness, uniqueness and individuality. Periodically, our separateness arouses feelings of being lost, and with the Greeks, we ask ourselves, "Whither do I go?" We wonder if there's a way home, longing with an undefinable desire to belong. Perhaps the purpose of our hectic, scrambled life, as we seek ever newer and greater stimulation and diversity, is to override and suppress that longing. When we finally stop to examine what we are doing, often our lives seem meaningless and bizarre.

This longing has been called "the spark of evolution" and represents the continuous thrust towards change, striving to reach the full expression of our greatest potential. Most of us sense that destiny but dimly, although we are certain of its imperative importance and glory. As our awareness of it increases, we become Seekers and thus we commence our journey home, our return. A solitary journey, it must be undertaken by each one of us separately for that destination must be experienced. Reading a travel book is very different from being there!

To find the answers we seek may seem both impossibly difficult and ridiculously simple for, truly, "what we seek with, is what we seek for" — that is, the spirit within us seeks to discover the all-pervading Spirit. The process, resulting ultimately in self-realization—the recognition of all that we are and always have been—is called surrendering and requires that we abandon or transcend our ego and that accumulation of pride, reason, rights, beliefs, petty concerns, relationships and material possessions that the ego incorporates. It entails an acceptance for the way things are, not for the way our ego-self believes they should be.

This does not mean dispensing with or negating all that we hold near and dear. But it does means letting go of our attachment to them and realizing that we no longer *need* them. It's alright to have them, but as we surrender, we lose the driving need to possess other people and things.

Surrender is a 'giving-over,' giving over our ego and will to the higher Power. Acknowledging our human helplessness to do it by ourselves, we give up and let God. St. Paul said, "Each day I die in Christ." As the ego dies, we leave our material attachments behind like a newborn chick leaving its shell, or a butterfly its cocoon. We are reborn.

God, Manitou, the Great Spirit, the personification of God in Jesus or Krishna, a piece of wood or stone, a totem, a statue, the sun, the moon—all are objects to which people have surrendered. I don't believe it matters exactly what we surrender to. It's the act of surrendering that is important. Surrendering, we remember who and what we really are. We know our Self once more and merge, flow, dissolve, meld, unite, become one with the Divine. In other words, we return to our eternal home, the place we never really left.

Each deep mystical experience I've had was preceded by a surrender of my will or ego. Others, when experiencing their enlightenment, also report the importance of their attitude of surrender.

For instance, Siddartha, who became the Buddha, thought, "I was born a Prince, surrounded with riches. I abdicated and abandoned my kingdom for the life of an ascetic seeking enlightenment. Seven years of rigors, poverty and self-torture brought me no closer although, in a coma from starvation, it brought me close to death. Studying scriptures, following the teachings of monks, hermits and sages did not give me the reward I sought. Now, I have done all I can do. I can do no more. Here, beneath this tree I will sit. Here I will stay. Here I will remain. Here I will be until my death — or until my enlightenment."

When he left his seat beneath that tree, he arose with the joy of self-realization — and changed the world!

Ramana Maharshi, who in a mysterious fashion taught me when I was seven years old, told of his enlightenment: "It happened when I was 17 and alone in my uncle's home in Madura. Previous to this I had not even had an interest in spirituality much less an inclination to dwell permanently in it. Although in good health, one day I had the thought; 'I am going to die!'. Following this realization, a violent fear of death swept through me. It did not occur to me to consult a doctor, or my elders, or my friends. I had to deal with the shock I'd received and the problem of death myself.

"I *surrendered* to the inevitability of my death. I went into it. I stretched out on the floor, imagining my death, my limbs stretched stiff as if *rigor mortis* had set in. I held my breath. "So now," I thought, "I'm dead, my stiff body will be carried to the burning ground and reduced to ashes. But what does death mean? Am I dead? Really dead? Do I not still have the full force of my being? Do I not hear the voice 'I am' still resonating within me and quite apart from my body?" Then I repeatedly asked myself, "What am I? What am I?"

"All fear of death evaporated. I surrendered to the depths of my being. That 'I', the One, the Self focused attention on itself with a powerful fascination. 'I' was the only real thing, the vivid living truth.

"Ever since, that 'I' has been present. Thinking, talking, eating, sleeping, walking, reading, it is continuously there like a deep continuous note underlying and blending with the symphony of all other notes. My absorption in the Self has remained unbroken ever since."

2500 years ago in India, it was commonly thought that each person possessed an atman, similar in concept to the individual soul. At that time, a great Reformation took place when the man we call the Buddha declared that "There is no atman." For many today, the declaration that there is no soul would be equally startling and, in fact, the Buddha's words provoked a great debate.

The Buddha was simply saying that there are not an infinite number of spirits, but rather, one single, all-pervasive Spirit and that each person, creature and material object is an expression of that Spirit. While water can appear in many forms — a summer cloud, a mountain stream, the morning dew on a rose, ice on a river or skating rink, a snowflake, a flood, a broad river, a gentle rain or a deluge — it's still H_2O, water. Similarly, while you and I see ourselves as separate and distinct personalities, in fact we are but different forms of the same unique Spirit.

There are two ancient Zen Buddhist stories from Japan, favorites of mine, which illustrate these concepts very nicely. The same stories are repeated by Sufis in Arabia and are similar to certain Hindu fables—an interesting "coincidence" which illustrates the interconnectedness of cultures and people around the world throughout history. The first is:

The Fish in the Water

Once upon a time, there was a school of little fish. They had just heard of water and, after arguing and philosophizing for many days as to whether such a thing actually existed, they decided to resolve the debate by asking the Great Fish.

In due course, after requesting and obtaining an audience, they said, "Oh, Great Fish, we have heard of water. If it exists, where can it be found and what is it?"

He answered, "You are created from water . . . you are born in water . . . you dwell in water . . . you breathe water. You are protected by water, surrounded by water, filled with water and strengthened and preserved by water. Every cell of your body, every atom of your being is composed of water. And when you die, you die in water and are returned to water."

Of course, they did not believe the Great Fish and, as they swam away through the ocean, they continued to argue as to whether such a thing as water might exist and to debate what it might be like.

Is there really a God or Divine Spirit, we may wonder, and, if so, where is it and what is it? The answer is as before: We are created in spirit . . . we are born in spirit . . . we dwell in spirit . . . we breathe spirit . . . and when we eat and drink, we eat and drink spirit. We move in spirit, are protected by it, surrounded by it, filled with it and strengthened by it. Every cell of our body, every atom of our being vibrates and glows with divine spirit. And when we die, we die embraced by spirit and return to spirit.

The second story again illustrates this theme —

The Doll of Salt

Once upon a time, there was a doll made of salt who lived in a toyshop. Along with the other dolls in the shop, she often pondered and discussed the nature of the ocean. After years of futile debate, the salt doll finally became weary of the exercise and determined to journey to the ocean to discover the truth for herself. Once there, she carefully waded in to experience the ocean's taste, feel and smell. Of course, she gradually dissolved. Only then, as her essence, her salt, merged with the essence, the salt of the ocean did she realize that she had always been an expression of the essence of ocean, even while she had the form of a doll.

The doll had searched and found her Self, and the essence she had searched for, she had searched with. Similarly, when we search for spirit, we search with spirit and discover and remember we are spirit. As spirit, our limits are unlimited, our boundaries unbounded. Like a pauper who inherited his father's vast fortune, everything becomes ours.

Ultimately, surrendering is like falling in love, where we let go of our judgements and control, and fall into a world of wonder, a state of intimate togetherness with our lover to the exclusion of all else. Similarly, when we surrender, we fall into the universe, into bliss, and into God. We cannot try to fall in love—it happens. We cannot try to surrender—it happens. When we do try, we become our own obstacles because it is impossible for the ego to surrender itself. To repeat, surrender occurs when we transcend our egos.

There are two ways of surrendering, comparable to the male and female role in sex. Sex, as the Hindus and Buddhists learned many centuries ago, can teach us the art of Surrender. While the teachings of this rich tradition, called Tantra Yoga, fill many volumes, I'd like to highlight one of its more pertinent concepts: The so-called feminine way is to be open, ready to accept and receive. The more passive way, it allows the ocean of consciousness to flow in and acts as a receptacle for the wine of the Divine Spirit. The more active, more assertive masculine way calls for a going into—leaping into the abyss, the void, nothingness. But whether our way is male or female, they both arrive at the same ocean of bliss, the same rapture.

During the sex act, we begin by controlling and continue to control and control until the time comes when we finally let go. Only then do we experience orgasm, becoming one with our partner. The sense of "me" disappears, the ego is gone, and we are completely in the present, merged with our lover and at one with the universe. Sex is the 'Kindergarten of Paradise.' Enlightenment is the ecstasy of the Cosmic orgasm.

While Tantric Yoga is the method of teaching union with the Divine through sex, and sex is a proper expression of love, Bhakti Yoga is union, a surrender, through love itself—love of the world and all its creatures and objects, love as taught by Jesus and expressed by St. Francis of Assisi.

St. Augustine, who achieved self-realization, said that there is but one rule to follow: "Love—and then do as you please!" Consider this solitary rule. Were we to love totally would not life be much more simple? What changes would it bring to our world? For instance, consider the highway signs that command "Drive Carefully" and the difference it would make were they to read "Drive Lovingly." Consider, too, all the "Thou Shalts" and "Thou Shalt Nots" of the Ten Commandments; were they to be substituted by the single commandment "Love," would the other Ten be necessary — or any other rule, command or law, divine or man-made?

St. Paul, in his letter to the Corinthians, has this to say about love:

"I will show you a more excellent way! If I speak in the tongues of men and of angels, but have not love, I am only a noisy gong or clanging cymbal.

If I have prophetic powers, and understand all mysteries and all knowledge, and if I have all faith, so as to remove mountains, but I have not love, I am nothing.

If I give away all I have, and if I deliver my body to be burned, but have not love, I gain nothing.

Love is patient and kind; love is not jealous or boastful;

Love is not arrogant or rude. It does not insist on

its own way; it is not irritable or resentful.

Love does not rejoice at wrong, but rejoices in the right.

Love bears all things, believes all things, hopes all things, endures all things.

Love never ends; as for prophecies, they will pass away; as for tongues, they will cease; as for knowledge, it will pass away.

Our knowledge is imperfect; but when the perfect comes, the imperfect shall pass away.

When I was a child, I spoke like a child, I thought like a child, I reasoned like a child; when I was a man, I gave up childish ways.

Now we see in a mirror dimly; but then, we shall be face to face. Now I know in part; then I shall understand fully, even as I have been fully understood.

So faith, hope, love abide, these three, but the greatest of these is love.

Before ending, I'd like to add a few other observations about surrendering. Studying what other people have written or said concerning their spiritual journey is useful to the extent that they may encourage our own search and confirm our own experiences. But trying to discover the presence of the Great Spirit through intellectualization is as futile as trying to catch the wind in our hands. Nor is the road to self-realization, as such enlightened beings as St. Francis and the Buddha discovered, through such harsh practices as self-flagellation, or denying our natural appetites or other self-tortures.

Techniques such as meditation, Jñana yoga, etc. which still the mind, are proper preparations for the experience of enlightenment. They lead us to the threshold, although the act of surrender itself, the crossing of that threshold, happens spontaneously:

> *As the illusion of the world,*
> *Like veils of morning mists, wears thin,*
> *Far distant doors of light swing wide,*
> *Inviting us to enter in.*

It happens. Suddenly, unexpectedly, like a flash of lightning, one moment you just are — and the next you are consumed by heavenly fire. One moment you are — and the next you have realized the Self, achieved enlightenment. You are drenched as if by a blessed rain, you are warmed as if by a blessed sun, your road ahead has been illuminated, you are returning Home, you are in unity with the Divine, you are One with All that Is.

Chapter 15

The Purpose of Life

A storm has blown in overnight and gale-driven rain lashes the windows. How lucky we are to have enjoyed yesterday's sunshine. I've arranged an early appointment at the university as well as a luncheon with my new girlfriend. Quietly I leave before Papa awakens.

When I return in mid-afternoon, Papa sets out a plate of cookies and hot chocolate and, at my request, plays his favorite symphonies—first one by Richard Strauss and then one by Gustav Mahler. The magic of the music casts its spell. Mystery becomes our companion and lost within ourselves we remain quiet for a long time after the music ends.

"This last year at university I started to wonder if there was any sense to life, any purpose. I more than half agreed with Shakespeare's statement that it was a tale full of sound and fury, signifying nothing. But when I hear music like that, I know there is some deep significance to it." I confess.

"I, too, went through those feelings when I was your age and at university," he admits. "University has that function, doesn't it? It starts one questioning."

"These past days with you have made me very aware of the spiritual side of things although I still don't know what the purpose of it all is. Have you figured it out? What do you think the purpose is? What are we here for?" I challenge.

"That's the big Why question, isn't it?"
he smiles . . .

We can answer some of our "how" questions; How did life evolve? —— some of our "what" questions; What is life? —— some of our "where" questions; Where is life found? —— and some of our "when" questions —— When were the earth and life created? But there are no satisfactory answers to all our "whys".

Why the earth? Why God? Why you? Why me? The persistent 'whys' of the young drive parents to distraction, for any attempt to answer merely leads to another unending series of imponderable whys. The final test paper for a philosophy course at a certain university asked only one question; "Why?" While other students wrote furiously for the allotted three hours, one student shrugged, scribbled and immediately handed in his paper. His was the only one that scored 100 percent. His answer consisted of one word: "Because."

While some say the only appropriate answer to the profound question, "Why?" is "Because" or, alternatively, "Why not?", such simplistic responses fail to address the persistent issues concerning our purpose in life, the reason for being. Many ideas and theories have been advanced which, in a very general way, can be summarized under three categories:

- There is the theory, first of all, that life has no meaning or purpose and is really just a "cosmic accident", a poor joke. This approach was espoused by the Epicureans of ancient Greece and has been echoed repeatedly in many guises—in the Book of Ecclesiastes, for example, and in such recent poetry and writings as Edward Fitzgerald's "The Rubaiyat of Omar Khayyam", Albert Camus' "L'Etranger", the fiction and essays of Jean Paul Sartre, and the existential philosophy of the Danish philosopher, Soren Kirkegaard. Life is short, they all imply, and when you're dead, you're dead.

This belief has led to two attitudes, one quite opposite to the other. One is to enjoy living as much as possible for it has little rhyme and less reason. The other attitude or philosophy is to wallow in morbidity and nihilism, defined in the Oxford dictionary as "a negative doctrine, the total rejection of religion or morals" and also known as the philosophy of nothingness—no purpose, no reason, no right, no wrong, no real joy. With this depressing philosophy, suicide appears to be a sane and reasonable action. Life is seen through very grim glasses.

- Opposing the Greek Epicureans were the Stoics who believed that the purpose of life was to do one's duty to oneself, one's family and one's country. These ideas were fully developed and handed down to us through the works of two Romans, Epictetus, a slave, and Marcus Aurelius, an emperor. Many religions and philosophies, from the laws of ancient Egypt to the Ten Commandments, from the ancient Shinto of Japan and the Chinese philosophy of Confucius to contemporary Calvanistic dogma, contain elements of Stoic thinking. This philosophy still plays a pertinent role today — witness the attention to duty in the work ethic of the Japanese factory worker and, in western society, the central importance of the Protestant work ethic to our very way of life.

- Yet, most of us feel that the extreme lifestyles of a wanton libertine, on the one hand, and an unsmiling puritan, on the other, are both unacceptable. Surely there is more to living than doing our duty or just having fun. The third general philosophical category addresses the middle ground—that there is something more, something with vast significance about our being here and that life has great mysterious importance. This third point of view, the spiritual, while valuing and incorporating much of the reasoned logic of both the Epicureans and the Stoics, values intuition and revelation as the ultimate source in defining our purpose and direction in life. "Know Thyself" commanded the unknown carver of those words over the entrance of the ancient Greek temple at Delphi. "An unexamined life is not worth living," said Socrates. "The Kingdom of Heaven is within," promised Jesus. Similar sentiments have been expressed by far eastern sages and illustrated with reports of enlightenment and self-realization.

While we may be instructed and encouraged by the teachings and reports of such people, we have only to refer to the highest authority in such matters—our own personal insights and mystic experiences—to be reassured of their validity. From my own "highest authority" and by what talents I have for observation and logical reasoning, I have come to believe that the purpose of life has six aspects. These (which, with intentional coincidence, all begin with the letter 'E') are: to Exist, to Enhance order, to Enjoy, to Experience, to Evolve and to achieve an Effect.

To Exist—To state that the purpose of life is to live may sound overly simplistic and obvious. Yet life is such a miracle, such a wonder, that it has its own justification—like a lovely bouquet of flowers which has no purpose other than to be beautiful; or like music; or like paintings and sculpture. John Keats said "Beauty is truth, and truth, beauty." The magnificence of life is it's own justification.

Picture in your mind, as a symbol of the will to exist, a solitary pine tree perched on the very brink of a cliff like we saw yesterday. Although its height is stunted, its base is thick, for it has been growing for a very long time. It shies away from the abyss, its branches growing lee of the tearing winds. Its roots are exposed by the continuous erosion of the cliff edge, but its rootlets tightly finger into every possible crevasse and fracture for support and suck what meagre sustenance they can from the barren rock. We observe the tenacity of life, the will, against all odds, to survive. We realize too how that will, that tenacity, that instinct for survival resonates and burns brightly within each one of us. Another dramatic symbol of survival is the leg trap which holds only the bloody severed paw of the escaped fox - what strength of will, what pain was endured to gnaw off its own leg to escape the trap and obey the imperious command to survive, to exist.

Every animal has a distinct talent for survival be it exceptional running, swimming, climbing, diving or flying or a particular behavior such as disguise, protective coloration, feigning death, or hiding to discourage or fool predators. Such adaptations, programmed into our very genes, ensure survival. Man's distinct talent is his ingenious brain.

Rare are the times that the edict to survive is set aside. Rarely do individuals self-destruct, commit suicide. The proverbial lemmings rush to perish in the sea. Obviously all do not commit suicide since lemmings continue to exist. We must assume that the majority die so the remainder will have sufficient food to survive. A further or higher principle can be discerned—the individual will voluntarily perish to preserve the existence of its family, tribe, race or species. The mother duck, faking a broken wing, lures the coyote away from her ducklings, occasionally enticing the hunter too near. The strongest baboons in a tribe attack a threatening leopard, sacrificing themselves for the preservation of their family. Man himself believes that the noblest of acts is to give one's life for another and immortalizes such deeds in legend and ballad. The command to exist as an individual is subservient to the higher hereditary command to preserve our progeny, to have our species continue to exist.

Nature is profligate. Only one acorn in tens of thousands reaches the stature of full grown oak. In other words, nature produces in an abundance to ensure a minority will survive. To nature it matters little that the majority perish, for nothing is really lost. What matters is race survival.

Suicide is committed for personal reasons only when the will to live is weakened by physical or mental illness. On the other hand, there is a proper time to die, a proper time to move on. With the approach of old age, when vitality begins to flicker, the will to survive sputters and fades. In primitive cultures, the old ones, sensing that their time has come, bid farewell to await death alone—the Inuit on the ice at night, the Japanese on the cold mountain, the African in the jungle. They will their death, the command to exist in the world having been satisfied at last. We, too, ultimately will choose our death.

My wife's ancient grandmother, incarcerated in the women's section of a nursing home, became increasingly sad, separated from her beloved husband of 70 years who was confined to the men's ward. Most days he visited her for a few minutes. Some days he forgot, for he, too, was in his nineties. One day she asked her son, who was visiting, to request that all her children and grandchildren visit her the next day. She explained that she was going to die the following night and wanted to say good-bye. Being a dutiful son he obeyed his mother, although he considered the request foolish as she was still in good health. During the next day, as her offspring came one by one to visit her, she quietly held the hand of each, looking long into each face and then, after requesting a kiss, whispered good-bye. The following morning she did not awaken from her sleep.

To Enhance Order—The Second Law of Thermodynamics states that all things wind down, that energy flows towards uniform dissipation throughout space, and that all higher organizations ultimately dissolve into a lesser state. That final state is called entropy.

I have always questioned this Law and in this I have good company, as Einstein doubted it as well. While the Law may be true with regard to the inorganic parts of the universe, it is decidedly untrue in respect of the organic parts. And if a law is not consistently true, then it is not a universal law. We know that life evolved from simple, one-celled organisms into ever more vastly complex forms, one of which is homo sapiens, you and me. Life is anti-entropy, in other words. An obvious purpose of life then is to continuously express ever greater complexity and order. Life opposes the dissolution of the universe, the falling of the ultimate starless night.

To Enjoy—If we had the power to create a perfect world, what would it be like? Surely it would contain all that is beautiful—rolling green hills and snow-capped mountains, pounding seas, and lazy, winding rivers and streams, miles of grassy plains, stark deserts, barren tundras, ice and snow. We'd probably introduce clouds to reflect the sun's rise and set, and storms to refresh and renew. And no doubt we'd create life in such variety as to challenge the numbers of stars in the universe, endowing each flower, plant and animal with its own exquisite beauty. As a final, loving touch, perhaps we'd order a large moon for the world's companionship as it whirled through the void of space.

Have we not just recreated the world we already have? What more could we need or wish for? Can we seriously doubt, as we find ourselves on this most beautiful of all planets, that it was made in order to be enjoyed—enjoyed in all its multitudinous aspects?

Enjoying life doesn't mean senselessly pursuing happiness, as the Epicureans advocated. True enjoyment of life is like listening to a glorious symphony. As we listen, we neither expect nor demand that the music become progressively better. Nor do we anticipate its climax. Each bar is important and enjoyed, each note an integral component of the whole, with discordant chords and minor keys illuminating the depths of the composition.

To Experience—I had a dream, not a very pleasant dream. I stood watching a poorly organized parade, a bedlam with the discordant notes of one marching band interfering with those of the next. And there were many floats, some gaudy and tinselled, others drab and dingy. Each float represented some facet of society. Occasionally someone would run from one float to another where they immediately became engrossed in the second float, ignoring the action of the parade as a whole. The closest depicted an office where men invested their lifetime and energy, and never counted the loss. Here were the floats of the housewife, the farmer, miner, poet; there, the drunk, the sport, the construction worker, the actor, the priest, the politician. Float after crowded float passed, the occupants games of power, greed or amusement and oblivious to all else.

Then I seemed to be looking down on the parade from a great height. I realized that it encompassed all mankind, and originated beyond the farthest horizon. In the other direction, I could see that it ended at the edge of a bottomless abyss into which all the floats and their occupants eventually tumbled. Very few left the parade before the end. Few even looked up from their activity and considered the possibility. Yet how precious those few who stood aside and let that mad parade go by. How few. How precious the few.

I recall an experience I once had, interviewing a geologist who had applied for an advertised position which required ten years' experience. After listening to him describe his background, I could not help blurting out, "You don't have ten years' experience, you have six months' experience repeated twenty times." We do not learn or grow when we stay on one 'float' and repeat the same thing over and over and over. Our exciting journey through life deteriorates into melancholy boredom.

In counselling I have often encountered people, quite different from that geologist, who are confused, stuck in life and depressed, having repeatedly failed in their many endeavors. They've been very ambitious and jumped from float to float, wanting to accomplish a whole series of major life goals. But before they've succeeded on even one float, they've been sidetracked, distracted by the charm of another. While we can't do everything at once, by concentrating on just one thing to completion, we experience success and then have the time to concentrate on the next goal. Step after step, goal after goal, we proceed on our way. Eternity invented time to allow us to follow all our dreams!

South of Phoenix, Arizona lies a range of arid hills sparsely covered by desert brush. The ancient Indian trails through that parched land are along dry, sandy creek beds. With friends I once travelled along these trails to where the empty stream-bed widened and a few trees grew. It was an obvious camping spot for there was wood for fire and the vegetation indicated the presence of water at shallow depth. Climbing the weathered cliffs, I discovered, carved in the rock, this inscription:

Paso por aqui

Coronado, 1512

It was easy to imagine how Coronado, the Spanish Conquistador, was led to this oasis by Indian guides and paused to refresh himself long enough to carve "I pass by here" before continuing his great journey to explore and discover the riches of a new world. Shortly afterwards, as my friends and I savoured the spell of that oasis and watched in awe as a spectacular sunset turned the cliffs into ever deepening hues of rose, I pondered those words.

I thought about how we all pass by here, this now, this moment, this life. As a man cannot enter the same river twice because it is always flowing and changing, so too it is impossible to pass by here ever again. Like Coronado, we can seize this moment, we can explore a new world and discover its riches both within and around us. We have only this one chance, this one moment in all eternity—our own special moment in time—to experience our glorious now. Life is not a dress rehearsal.

To Evolve—Rockets sent to probe our solar system have revealed that highly evolved life forms are found only on the third planet. As we observe the near infinity of space with its hundreds of thousands of millions of stars in our home galaxy and pause to consider that, across the universe, there are a vast number of galaxies, each with their billions of stars, and then contemplate how many stars have a multiple planetary system, we must believe that somewhere, somehow, other forms of life exist. What different forms we cannot begin to imagine. Life in the universe, however, is rare, perhaps as rare as one planet per galaxy. Human life is even rarer—we are a unique species to be found only on this world. Rare, and precious.

What a marvellous, infinite variety of organisms have evolved since life first originated on this earth! When we view this fantastic conglomeration we may wonder, at first, if there is any pattern to it all, or whether all these life forms are merely a wide-ranging chaotic assemblage. A pattern can be discerned, however, when we consider the steady progressive evolution of species towards ever higher states of consciousness. Man, the most highly evolved of all animals, stands at the apex of evolution's thrust towards consciousness for obviously we are more aware than a dog which is more aware than an alligator which is more aware than a fish which is more aware ... and so it goes down the evolutionary scale.

Julian Huxley added to Darwin's theory of evolution the concept of "survival of the fittest"—only the strongest survive while the weak perish. With this was created the mistaken notion that the ideal evolutionary survivor is a powerful aggressive beast that kills and destroys in its headlong rush through life. On the contrary, as ever more complex life forms with ever greater consciousness have evolved, love has played an ever greater role.

The lone wolf soon perishes, for example, but the wolves in a wolf pack survive as they cooperate, protect and care for each other and their offspring. Frogs, by comparison, are halfway back along evolution's path and exhibit no capacity for love. They do not protect their eggs and newly born tadpoles must fend for themselves. Human babies are unique, remaining quite helpless and in need of feeding and loving care for several years. This lengthy time period allows mankind's accumulated skills and wisdom to be passed on. Thus our greater ability to love allows us to progress. They survive best who love best.

How quickly our species, homo sapiens, has progressed and continues to develop! To better grasp the notion of that accelerated climb, let's compress the past three and a half or four billion years of life on earth into a short two-month period. By this measure, it was only a week ago that organisms evolved to a sufficiently complex stage with shells that could be preserved as fossils. Just four days ago fish began to swim in the oceans. Yesterday dinosaurs roamed the landscape. Sixteen hours ago, the first prairies emerged and were inhabited by vast herds of mammals while modern birds flew overhead. And just this morning, man's distant primate forefather appeared. Our own arrival was so recent and sudden that I doubt whether the universe has had time to notice. Half an hour ago, the earliest man-like creatures stepped onto the world's stage, inventing skin clothing, weapons and art as they continued to evolve. Barely 40 seconds ago, modern man—discoverer of fire, domesticator of animals, inventor of farming, writing, civilization, Bingo and the Quantum Theory—showed up on the scene. One second ago, the Normans were invading England. Half a second later, Columbus set sail for America and in the few remaining milliseconds since, all of the events of modern history —

from the settling of the Americas to World War II, the development of nuclear energy and the start of our exploration of outer space—have taken place.

Although we are comparative strangers, newcomers, we already dominate our planet. Most other dominant species have lasted for hours or even days on our compressed time scale, evolving into more complex forms during their time on earth. Geologically, as a dominant life form, we can expect to be around for millions of years and to continue evolving—to such an extent, perhaps, that future man may not recognize us as his primitive ancestor. What will we become?

Evolution will continue as it always has, and new species (perhaps with man's help and the skills of genetic engineering) will come into existence. But now that nature has created an animal conscious of itself, evolution will undoubtedly continue and accelerate in the direction of greater consciousness and increased awareness, endowing our descendants with ever greater capacities.

These capacities will not only include greater understanding and control of our environment with our ever increasing technology but an enhanced perception of our place in the scheme of things. With our ever expanding awareness we sense a rhythm; the rhythm of the seasons; the regular migration of birds across uncharted skies; the orderly decay of radioactivity; the rotation of that vast galactic wheel we call the Milky Way. Everywhere we discern patterns, rhythms, fractals, harmonies and orders. If there is pattern, rhythm, harmony, and order, we accept that there is intelligence at work. What is that intelligence? What is its purpose? Searching for an answer, we encounter mystery beyond mystery beyond mystery. Slowly we understand. Slowly the mysteries dissolve.

Even now we have the ability and techniques to accelerate the evolutionary trend. Even now we can be more than we are. Earlier in this chapter we discussed the

Stoic belief that the purpose of life was to do one's duty. Since then, governments, churches and every other institution invented by man have defined, to their own advantage, what they stipulate that duty to be. On the contrary, is not our first responsibility to concentrate on our personal growth and development? By loving more, by using techniques that enhance our consciousness, including Jñana Yoga and meditation, our awareness will increase until we experience an evolutionary shift and achieve personal enlightenment. And when we touch the eternal, we will know ourselves for the first time.

The Effect—Imagine that we are at the base of an exposed cliff or outcrop of naked white limestone, a coquina, full of shells of one particular species. As we climb the cliff, we observe that all the shells are identical and realize that during the tens of thousands of years they were accumulating, the species underwent no evolutionary change. We climb a little further and notice that a few of the shells appear different and that, just above these few, all the shells are changed. Some evolutionary adaptation has occurred, not gradually but abruptly—almost instantaneously, in fact.

This kind of jump or quantum leap is characteristic of evolution. Life forms remain the same for long periods and, while mutations constantly occur, it is only when one mutant evolves which is an improvement and better adapted to the environment, that the whole species changes. One individual leads the way. The rest follow.

By the same token, it matters terribly what we as individuals do, for it is always the individual—the Jesus, the Buddha, the Freud, the Shakespeare, the Picasso, the Einstein—who leads humanity in a new direction. We too, can make a difference. We too, want our life to matter. As creation is an organic whole, when any change occurs, the whole is changed. As we change, the effect will resonate through the cosmos. We can weave our mystery into the tapestry of the universe.

How precious, how important are we? We are not an improbable accident, a freak among the cold, uncaring stars. Through our awareness, the galaxy, like a newborn baby, is becoming aware of itself for the first time. We are the eyes of the universe, its sole organ of consciousness. We are treasured as we treasure our very eyesight. We are the ultimate reason for the existence of the cosmos.

St. Paul said, "The universe waits breathless for the realization of man." We shouldn't keep it waiting much longer.

Chapter 16

The Good, the Bad and the Ignorant

I phone home to inform my parents I will return the day after next and ask them to meet my plane. I don't want to talk about it on the phone but when Dad asks if I've accepted the job he arranged for me and I tell him I haven't, he becomes angry. He says I have to. Then I, too, get angry and shout things which I know I'll later regret.

As I join Papa, I'm in a vile mood and mumble under my breathe, "Guess I'm old enough to make up my own mind. Don't need him to tell me every little thing I should do."

Wisely Papa keeps silent. Words are scarce during breakfast. Slowly my anger subsides. I am surprised at how violently I reacted to both the thought of taking the job and my father's demands. At least I now know my decision about the job, and I realize I have to make up my mind what I am going to do instead. But not right this minute. This is the time to be with Papa.

I sheepishly grin an apology, and say, "I'm sorry tomorrow is our last day together. You've been more than a loving grandfather. You've been my teacher. Although I'm not positive about where I'm going with my life — that's what I was arguing about with Dad — you've been more help than I can tell you. Our visit's been great on many levels. But I don't know, Papa, what it is — I have this funny feeling inside, in the pit of my stomach. I can't figure out what it is. It's not exactly disappointment but it is an empty, sorta let down feeling as if I've missed or lost something."

"Perhaps it's like the feeling a little child has when it discovers there's no Santa Claus?" he suggests, smiling.

"I don't think I understand what you mean." After

I realize he isn't going to make any further comment, I add, "I'll think about it."

Then I continue, still with a residue of anger, "Changing the subject, Papa, you seem to hold a viewpoint where 'God's in His heaven, all's right with the world.' It just isn't realistic. My life's not perfect. Don't think anyone else's is either. On T.V. we see starved babies, their empty stomachs bloated. We see killings, wars, atrocities. I even read where, among the poor in South America, parents maim their own children to ensure better luck as beggars. Closer to home, it's no better. Our papers are full of murders and scandals. I just don't get it. You don't have your head in the clouds. You're practical and you've succeeded on the world's terms. But what do you do about the ugly stuff, the suffering of others and all that evil? How do you reconcile those things? Do you just ignore it? I don't see how you can; there's just too much wrong. The world's a mess."

"I look at it this way . . .

In the beginning God created heaven and earth as an expression of Him/Her/Itself. What sort of place was created? Peering as far as we can into the infinitesimal, using electron microscopes, we marvel at the intricacies of perfection disclosed. Peering as far as we can into the infinite, using arrays of radio telescopes, we again marvel at the panorama of perfection that unfolds there. Astronauts declare our planet, a blue and white orb glowing against the black void of space, to be the loveliest object in the firmament. It is our one and only home. But, if God created earth, then why is not the world perfect? Why are there evils, suffering?

The Creator, the Bible states, created man in His own Image, which means that we are also creators. We create our society, our arts and sciences, our technologies and industries, all the things that make up our civilization and our way of life. We dominate, have dominion over the planet. Unfortunately, too often we forget that having dominion also implies caring for the planet, looking after it and not despoiling it, ravishing it. We pollute our air, we poison our waters. Life forms in great numbers die, extinguished forever. At times we murder each other, hurt without pity, terrorize the helpless, torture our victims and brutalize ourselves. God created Paradise. Man created Hell.

Are we then evil, wretched creatures full of sin? First, let's define some terms: right, wrong; good, bad; evil, the Devil; and finally sin.

Right is that which works. We've made the right connections if the radio and television work. We know we've made the right choice when we feel happy and loved and feel worthwhile to ourselves and to others.

Wrong is that which does not work. We've made a wrong choice if we feel lonely, frustrated, unhappy and unsuccessful. We can all agree readily that these feelings are bad for we feel neither loved nor loving, nor worthwhile to ourselves or anyone else. When we feel this way, it's time to ask what we can change to obtain the good feelings that we so earnestly desire.

Good is that which enhances our health, happiness and wisdom and *Bad* is the opposite and brings us 'down' — disease, sadness and depression.

Evil is the act of hurting — ourselves or someone else. Evil is not facing our own pain and anger but putting our pain out there onto someone or something else. A person, abused as a child, too often, in turn, will abuse others. The remembered anger and pain is not accepted and responsibly dealt with, and instead it is expressed again and again. Other examples — The thief: "I rob you because I am poor." The envious: "I am jealous of you because of what I lack." The killer: "I hate you because I fear." The vicious: "I hurt you because I hurt."

When our angers and pains are repressed, denied, not responsibly dealt with, and kept within, they become directed onto ourselves; we experience dis-ease, sickness. Medical doctors refer to this as the psychosomatic aspect that is inherent in all illnesses. If our repressed hurting and anger are severe, the evil intense, our disease can kill us. Reported miracle cures occur when we abruptly stop hurting ourselves and release our evil, our anger. In earlier times such healings were referred to as "a casting out of demons" — the casting out of the evil within.

When we fail to accept responsibility for our own pain, we feel helpless, powerless, frustrated, and more and more angry. *Violence* is the ultimate expression of that helplessness, that impotence. So much impotency exists in the world. So much violence. So much evil.

The Devil is simply evil personified. Evil becomes The Evil One, The Evil, D'Evil, the Devil and what a wonderful excuse that gives us for not taking responsibility. "It's not my fault; the Devil made me do it!" Or, better yet; "The Devil did it!"

And what is *Sin*? When I was young any behavior that was considered to be less than desirable was called a sin. Sin was a very popular topic of conversation. Complaints and criticisms invariably commenced with such words as, "It's just a sin that the government doesn't . . .", or "I think it's a sin the way she carries on or wears or talks, . . . etc", or "It's a sin that we can't afford this or that."

At this time, in the mid 1920's, it was a dictate of society that church be attended twice on Sunday, both morning and evening. In the case of children, it was three times as they were also obliged to attend Sunday School in the afternoon to improve their sinful little souls. Church was a torture for the young. Dressed in their stiff Sunday best, they were chastised if they squirmed with irritation or aching boredom. My Sunday best was a thick blue serge suit, always in need of brushing for it had a static attraction to dust and lint. This suit caused me great agony for I was allergic to wool and invariably, by Sunday night, I had developed a flaming, itching rash. Even a schoolday was better than a Sunday.

Dr. Harbinson, our minister, lived with his housekeeper in the square brick manse at the top of our street. (No scandal was ever attached to that arrangement.) His upright, rigid figure was rarely glimpsed other than on Sundays, and when he did appear on the street, he responded with a distant haughty nod to the reverent greetings of his flock. I always ran when passing his house.

On Sundays, his personality changed. No longer taciturn, the long prayer alone could extend for 15, 20, even 25 minutes as he tattled to God about our sins and shortcomings. His sermons were always about the Hell fire and Damnation that awaited us, his square-cut grey beard trembling with indignation at our wickedness, his watery-pale blue eyes blazing his hatred and anger, and his pointing, accusing finger probing the air like a poker stirring the unquenchable fires of Hades.

I was confused by the complete contrast between these church sermons where God was an unforgiving, wrathful, vengeful judge who had designed everlasting tortures for our sinful souls and the Jesus of Sunday School, who was also God, but was a sissy sort of person who talked about kindness and goodness and forgiving everybody. Perhaps the confusion in my mind started me thinking. For instance, I wondered how the minister knew that he alone was going to go to heaven because it seemed to me that my Mom and Dad were okay and should also be able to make it.

What has happened to sin since that time? How things change. No longer is sin on the tip of our tongues and no longer are we living in perpetual fear and holy terror that all our thoughts and actions are sinful. Except in the case of evangelical, fundamentalist groups it is only infrequently talked about, even in church. So what happened?

First, the government took it over. Just as the government has taken over the responsibility for our education, our health, our welfare, and intrudes into every corner of our lives, so it has taken over sin and legislated against it, making it illegal, a crime.

Formerly, the sinner who ignored or broke the precepts of proper moral behavior was ostracized by society and condemned by the church. Now he was a criminal who broke the law and suffered its penalties. Our language also changed to reflect this new approach. While we still object to and complain of the same things as before, all of our expressions such as "I think it's a *sin* that ..." have changed to "I think it's a *crime* that ..." Sin has disappeared and crime flourishes. Sin has been forgotten to such an extent that many think the word SIN is simply an abbreviation for Social Insurance Number.

Our concepts have continued to change and our perception of crime, in turn, has taken a curious twist. What was originally a sin, and then a crime, is now too often seen as merely a Social Problem. Thus, the former sinner or criminal becomes a product of 'Society's Failure'. Regardless of the violence of the crime or the suffering of the victim, it is no fault of the perpetrator but, rather, is entirely the fault of the government for not providing a better life and greater opportunities in the first place. This perversion of reasoning condemns society as the sinner and sympathizes with the criminal, the innocent victim of society's shortcomings.

There is a modern day update to the Bible story of the Good Samaritan. While travelling along a road (now a street), our modern day Good Samaritan (a Psychiatrist), discovers a man lying in a ditch (now a back alley). The man has fallen among thieves and has been sorely beaten, robbed and left for dead. (Nothing has really changed, so far, has it?). Our modern Samaritan, however, does not pick up the dying man, take him to a luxury hotel, obtain medical help and pay all the bills. No, today our Good Samaritan says to himself, "I must find the men who did this. They *really* need my help!"

Although for humor's sake, that story may be an exaggeration, it still points out a certain contemporary attitude. While this attitude is wrong, not taking any responsibility for what goes on in society is equally wrong. Society is you, me — all of us, including the criminal. The criminal is entirely responsible for his crime, his sin. We are entirely responsible for not only ourselves but also the world in which we live. We made it the way it is. Fortunately, we have the power not only to change present conditions, but also the skills of psychology to heal the scars we carry from the suffering and abuses of the past.

Sin can be defined as not taking responsibility. A common attitude is believing, "I can't help it; nothing I can do about it; it's not my fault". By not accepting responsibility for our own deeds, words, thoughts, and attitudes, we try to escape any feeling of sin and to have an excuse to act irresponsibly. All too often, with this wonderful excuse, too many of us see no reason to honor commitments to either ourselves or others and consequently fail to achieve our desires and goals.

A further problem is that, in spite of our irresponsibility and our excuses for lack of achievement, we still sense, deep down, that we really are responsible and that we can be more than we are. We sense there is a great purpose to our being here, as we previously discussed. God sentenced us to life. How, we wonder, are we serving our sentence? When we examine our shortcomings or sins, the same old feelings of guilt and shame arise again, and we are right back where we started, although the problem is much worse than before. In the old days when sin was so popular and plentiful, we were all regarded as sinners. Similarly repentance of one's sins was an every day affair and forgiveness was freely given to the repentant. Not today. Today our feelings of sin, no longer popular or acceptable to polite society, are hidden, and being hidden and suppressed and not forgiven, our inner stresses fester and magnify, providing a good living for armies of psychiatrists, psychologists, and social workers.

Will we not change the world when we take responsibility for ourselves — for what we do, say, think and feel? Will we not change the world when we stop blaming others for what they do, or for the way things are? Objecting to pollution, are we still consuming the products whose manufacture caused that pollution? Detesting violence, have we dealt with our own pain? Sick, when will we face our own anger and shame? The responsibility lies with you and me — not with our governments, our corporations, our unions, our parents, a virus or "them" or anything else "out there".

While sin has been a 'Big Seller' in western religions we find, surprisingly, that it is absent in eastern religions. Buddhism, Hinduism — these eastern sects believe that the actions we call sins or crimes are merely expressions of our ignorance. Ignorance, to their way of thinking, means not knowing the answer to the question "What am I?", and not remembering our divine source. Thus we act as if we were each solitary individuals rather than expressions of the One Divine Spirit. From their point of view, the robber robs himself for he is ignorant of what he is and what we all are together. Furthermore, a killer can neither kill nor be killed, for we are all eternal.

It has been said, "The world judges us by our actions. We judge ourselves by our intentions." In other words, society may judge our actions and motives to be good or bad, right or wrong, successful, helpful and altruistic or a failure, sinful, evil or criminal. On the other hand when we examine our motives or intentions, we find that we never have more than two: to give love and to receive love. Have any of us ever wished to do less than our best? — the best for love of ourselves, our family, our friends? — and to receive our loved one's love in return? Certainly there is no sin in that! Of course, in hindsight, later events may well prove that what we did was not the best course of action. Such action was due to our ignorance and ignorance according to eastern religions, is neither crime nor sin. Based on the facts available at the time and with logic and reasoning based on these facts, doesn't each of us always make what seems the best possible choice?

Let's ask ourselves again. Have we ever done anything that we did not hope would make us feel good about ourselves and result in more love and appreciation from others? Too often we forget and say, "Oh, if I'd only known, I certainly would have done things differently". But we didn't know. We did our best, but were ignorant of all the facts and factors. When we remember this, we realize the futility of beating ourselves up and feeling guilty, wrong, sinful or evil for the way things turned out. Let the past bury the past!

If sins are merely ignorance, isn't ignorance something we can forgive? And is not SIN simply an abbreviation for Self-Inflicted Nonsense?

If we accept we always wanted to do and be the best possible, we can assume others do the same. Sometimes others' actions seem pretty strange to us and the actions of people such as terrorists or child molesters, even stranger, more perverted. We say, "I just don't understand how people can act that way. They're weird!" But if we honestly examine their motives, we find that their wants are the same as our own: giving or asking for love. The terrorist may be expressing love for his country and asking for the approval and the love of his fellow fanatics. Similarly, the child molester expresses his/her need for love although in a bizarre, objectionable fashion.

Of course such behavior and acts are unacceptable and repugnant, as are all acts which result in pain to others. Society rightly takes action to constrain such deeds and prevent their recurrence. However, we need not condemn the person for he/she acts with the same loving motives as you and I, and we understand the *action* as due simply to ignorance. We do, however, refuse to allow them to continue to act that way. But by accepting that everyone's ultimate motive is love, there seems to be no sin to forgive. *Ignorance* itself is forgivable.

To repeat, this does not mean that we must accept and blindly approve of all the actions, words or deeds of another. That person who is an alcoholic, a thief, a cheat, a wife beater or a killer is still entirely responsible for what he does. But the doer is not the deed; the actor is not the act. We must differentiate. The doer, the actor, wants only to love and to be loved and to feel worthwhile. The deed, the act, may be bizarre, hurtful, destructive and entirely unacceptable. However, we can accept the doer or actor as an expression of the Divine and understand the deed or act as merely an expression of ignorance. Perhaps we can learn to say (to ourselves), "I refuse to be angry and resent or hate you for you are a pure and perfect spirit like myself; but I also know from your actions — you're crazy!"

Simple, isn't it? Of course not! We have been carrying our resentments, hates, hurts, rejections and betrayals for such a long time that they now seem part of us. But when we forgive, who benefits? The one forgiven may not even know he or she is forgiven, but we know! Those heavy burdens are taken from *our* shoulders. We are freed; freed of the past, freed to go ahead with our life. Let's do ourselves a favor: forgive. And when we do, we shall see the world anew, in all its perfection.

After a friend of mine was robbed, she said, "I guess he needed the things more than I do, so I freely give them to him." That way she did not have to suffer feelings of being ripped off or hurt and instead remained peaceful and loving.

Another example: Hospitalized after being imprisoned, repeatedly raped and beaten for two days, the girl uttered no word of anger or complaint. Upon inquiry concerning her strange behavior, she said, " He held me for two days. That is enough! I forgive him and refuse to let him hold me one second longer."

Jesus equated forgiveness with healing and used the terms interchangeably. Sometimes he merely touched the sick; other times he said, "Take up thy bed and walk," other times, simply "Thy sins are forgiven." In each case, healing occurred. An update version could be "Forgive your ignorance, forget your S.I.N., your self-inflicted nonsense and be free of guilt and all disease".

He also taught us that all things are forgiven man, but one; he is not forgiven who blasphemes the Holy Spirit. To blaspheme means to speak badly about or deny. When we deny the power and glory of the Spirit within us by uttering nonsense such as, "I can't do it", or "I'm too old, young, scared, or weak", or "It wasn't my fault, I couldn't help it", or "I don't have the time, education, intelligence, or money", and act like the helpless victim and wretched sinner we imagine ourselves to be, do we not negate, deny and blaspheme the all knowing, all powerful Holy Spirit within us? Such self-inflicted nonsense truly becomes unforgivable.

When we remember what we are, it is as if we had never forgotten and, in ignorance, blasphemed our holy spirit. When the light shines, the darkness is forgotten, it's as if it had never existed. When we remember that our spirit shines, it's as if we never left eternity. No self-inflicted nonsense, no ignorance, no words, no deeds, no denials, no thoughts can ever change or dim that pure and perfect Spirit that we eternally are. We are very holy. We are the beloved children of God.

Chapter 17
The Bardo

To create a festive atmosphere for our last evening together, I wear a silk embroidered shirt I purchased on a trip to Mexico and Papa wears a purple shot-silk shirt from Thailand. We dine at his favorite restaurant but save dessert for our return, large slabs of homemade chocolate cake.

"I want to thank you, Papa. I've had such a good time. I feel I'm a different person than I was two weeks ago. I'm feeling energetic and excited about what's ahead. Although I regret the visit's over, I can hardly wait to get going with my plans," I tell him.

"Oh? and what happened to your feelings of yesterday, feeling disappointed and empty or that something was missing?"

"You were right. There's no Santa Claus," I grin.

"Good! and ...?"

"And there's no mentor, no guru, no one but myself to give me what I want. You said it time and time again. Now, I understand. Only I can do it."

"Right! There's no tooth fairy, no fairy godmother with a magic wand, not even an Easter bunny to give us a chocolate egg," Papa laughs.

"But, like you said, it's all there for me — much more than I ever guessed. And I've decided."

"Congratulations!" he smiles.

"I have to work out several things first but don't be surprised if I return in a few months."

"That would be wonderful!" he exclaims putting an arm around my shoulder.

Somehow our hands clasp each other's and we

gaze into each other's eyes. How precious our days together have been. How I love my Papa. My tears well up and almost overflow. I can't properly describe what happens next. One moment, I'm staring at him. Then, suddenly, his face disappears and I am staring into a light, a blinding light, a brilliant radiance. It lasts only an instant, an earth-shattering instant. My voice unsteady, I tell Papa I don't understand and ask him what he had done.

"I didn't do anything. But I am aware that something happened. Tell me about it."

I do, as best as I can. He then explains, "Accept that what happened was your personal insight. You saw me as the pure and perfect spirit that I am, which is the same pure and perfect spirit that you are and everyone else is. It was your insight. Not mine. Yours. Yours alone. I've known others to have similar experiences. Unfortunately, too often they idolize or worship the one they saw transfigured. Unscrupulous gurus encourage such belief and take advantage of it. So know it was your heightened awareness alone that allowed you to see beyond the material world."

"At least, Papa, let me acknowledge it's been our conversations that increased and expanded my awareness so that it could happen. And thanks for one more lesson."

He raises his eyebrows in a silent question. What have I missed or got wrong? It takes a moment or two before I understand. "I guess it wasn't 'one more lesson' was it, Papa? I guess it's the same lesson, the same lesson you've been repeatedly trying to teach me time after time throughout my visit."

His face beaming his approval, he gives me a warm hug saying, "I love you, Robert." I almost cry once more.

After taking several minutes to regain my

composure, I tell him, "I've been wondering, Papa, what last question to ask you. The most profound one I can think of is: What happens after death?"

"Even the Buddha refused to answer that question for his disciples. He implied we'd all find out soon enough," he chuckles.

"Then is it proper for me to ask you?"

Nodding his consent, he replies . . .

It's natural, as we observe the death of others and face the inevitability of our own demise, to wonder, "What happens after death?" and ask, like the ancient Greeks, "Whither do we go?" A generation or two ago, sex was a taboo subject, not to be discussed in polite company, while death and dying were common topics of conversation. Today, sex is freely discussed, but death has become taboo, something to be whispered about and all evidence of it hidden as quickly as possible. Yet is it not still the great mystery, the fearful unknown? And are we not still intrigued by it? Would it not, in fact, be easier to understand life if we had some idea of what happened after life? Many answers and philosophies have been proposed.

Ancient scribes — Herodotus, the Greek devotee of the secret Egyptian "Mysteries of Antiquity," and Plato in Book 12 of the Republic, to name but two, seem to have delved much more into these matters than us, their descendants. Death was not considered a morbid subject but a fascinating mystery whose study had a practical value. They pondered, "While we know that eventually we will all die, few learn how to die. If we learn how to die, will we not know how to live?"

Socrates, 2,500 years ago, pointed out that there are two possible fates that await us—the first is that there is nothing after death, in which case death might be compared to a pleasant dreamless sleep; and the second is that there is another form of existence, sure to be better than this life. In either case, he concluded, there is nothing to fear from death.

Many believe in the first alternative—that when you're dead, you're dead, and your only hold on immortality is what you pass on to your children through your genes. The majority, however, prefer to think that some essence survives death—be it a soul, a spirit, or an atman which goes to Heaven, Paradise, Valhalla, the Blessed Isles or the Land of the Dead, if one has led a "good" life. According to some thinking, anyone whose earthly behavior wasn't "good enough" will find himself in everlasting Hell or, alternatively, in Purgatory, a temporary Hell, if his sins warrant only a few millennia's worth of punishment. Some believe that we remain dead until we rise from our graves on Judgement Day when a few select will go to Heaven while the rest of us will be damned to Hell forever.

Most cultures worldwide, however, believe in some form of reincarnation, the theory that one has repetitive rebirths into lifetimes after lifetimes. They believe that when we are reborn or reincarnated, the status of our new life will be commensurate with the goodness of our previous existence. Rebirths go on and on until the soul evolves into a perfect state. A majority vote in favour of this theory does not constitute proof, of course. On the contrary, there seem to be good arguments against it.

The first is simple arithmetic. A curious fact: the total number of humans who have ever lived since Adam and Eve is estimated at 22 billion. Over five billion, almost one quarter of the total, are on the face of the planet today! That is the measure of our population explosion. Mathematically then, the average number of former lives each soul could have had is three and a claim to having had dozens or even hundreds of former human lives is improbable. Because of this, there is validity to the Hindu saying that, "Human birth is a rare and precious thing and should be treasured deeply."

To date, the rarity of life is confirmed by our explorations of the solar system. We appear to be alone and Mars, which was considered to be the most probable candidate for extraterrestrial life, is even devoid of bacteria, life's most primitive form. Because life is so rare, a belief has arisen in India and elsewhere that souls in great numbers are sort of "waiting in line" to be reborn and some spirits, more impatient than others to return to life, may appear as ghosts or try to possess another soul's body, often in the guise of being a friendly "guide." Obviously, according to Hindus, such things should be strictly avoided.

A second argument against reincarnation necessitates some understanding of that very strange thing we call time. The dictionary is of little help for it defines time as "duration" or "continued existence" which are merely synonyms. Time was invented by Man as a way to measure the rate of changes he observed in and around himself. Different cultures consider time differently. We, in our Western culture, view time as linear—running from beginning to end. The Indians in North America viewed it as circular for each season repeated the cycle of the previous year. Others view time as a spiral where we almost but never quite repeat. Nor is time absolute or constant. We may sometimes say, "Time went fast" or, on the contrary that, "Time seemed to drag on and on."

Mr. Einstein has told us that time is relative, that it depends on our point of view. The greater the velocity, the more time slows. If a space ship radios back to earth the ticking of a clock, the ticks are heard further and further apart as the velocity of the ship increases. If the spaceship finally reaches the velocity of 186,000 miles per second or the speed of light—the next tick never comes. Time has slowed to a stop. Is this not our definition of eternity—where there is no time?

Our mind boggles when we try to understand time rationally. While the spaceship is in eternity from the point of view of the citizens on earth, in the spaceship itself the clock still ticks merrily away measuring time for the astronauts as before. An even more difficult concept to grasp is the notion that anti-matter can be considered to be the same as other matter except that, for anti-matter, time runs backwards (whatever that means!).

An analogy for time may help. Imagine we are in a helicopter hovering over the ocean some distance offshore and filming the waves below. Later, as we view the film, we see the waves crest and trough, sparkling in the sunlight, while a seagull is silhouetted, floating up and down on the water. Now let's play the film backwards. There is no change in the picture. The same seagull bobs in the background and the waves come and go, as before. In fact, as we play the film back and forth, we actually forget which direction is forward or backward for they are identical. In both cases we see the eternal ocean with its eternal waves. To the individual waves, time exists, but to eternity where time does not exist, everything happens now.

We as individuals, like solitary waves, exist in time and space, but from the point of view of eternity, the point of view of God, all is One where everlasting waves come and go, come and go. The past is now. The future is now. And the Great Spirit eternally incarnates. Thus, "I" am now a Pharaoh, an astronaut, a Crusader, a galley slave, an accountant, a serf, Napoleon, all people, all things, all interconnected, all multiple expressions of the One organic Whole. Perhaps those who claim to remember a former life, a former incarnation, are merely "tuning in" to one of "Our" shared experiences, one of the other waves.

Over 100 years ago, Henry David Thoreau wrote these lovely words about time in his book "Walden Pond".

Time is but a stream I go a-fishing in.
I drink from it; but as I drink
I see how shallow it is.
The thin stream slips silently away;
But eternity remains.
I would drink deeper!
I would fish those waters
Whose bottom is pebbled with stars!
I know not One;
I know not the first letter of the alphabet.
I have always regretted I was not as wise
As the day I was born.

No book sheds more light on the after-life than the *Bardo Thödol*, the Tibetan Book of the Dead. The handwritten copies of this strange book, invariably illuminated with intricate designs and paintings of mandalas and angelic and demonic figures, appear on casual reading, to be exotic Tour Guides. Tour guides of the "Bardo", the place where the soul finds itself after death. In Tibetan Buddhism, the main duty of the lamas is not in teaching the Dharma, the Truth revealed by the Buddha, nor is it in conducting various religious ceremonies nor officiating at births and weddings. Their main function is much more important—guiding the soul of the dead through the "Bardo".

As a text book, an instructional manual, it contains directions on how to allow the dying to let go of life and die in peace, with specific instructions for physically pressing on various nerve centres to close the door of the womb of rebirth. Included, too, are descriptions of the powers and limitations one has while in the Bardo, along with invocations and prayers for the soul's protection while in this state and many severe warnings about what to avoid as well as dire predictions for those who fail to heed these warnings. This curious "Tour Guide" leads the dead through the Bardo to the soul's destination, that destiny being either rebirth in the world or liberation and union with the Divine.

The *Bardo Thödol* is much more than a simple, literal, or esoteric interpretation would indicate. There is a deeper meaning, an esoteric or symbolic interpretation, particularly in the section regarding reincarnation. Carl Jung, the great Psychologist, fascinated by the insights of the book, wrote a commentary in which he contrasted the deep psychological and spiritual understanding of the *Bardo Thödol* with the "spiritualistic literature of the West which again and again gives one a sickening impression of the utter inanity and banality of communications from the spirit world."

The Tibetan Book of the Dead was committed to writing around 700 B.C. but its source or sources were much earlier and Indian in origin. If the after-death experiences that it describes are true, we may wonder who wandered through that strange realm and returned to tell of it. The probable answer is that the book is a compilation from many mystical, visionary experiences as well as the "after-life" experiences of those who were "clinically dead" and subsequently continued to live.

Much has been made of similarities with other texts—for instance, the Judgement scene is almost identical to both the Judgement scene in the Egyptian Book of the Dead and the Judgement scene in Plato's Republic. I suggest the commonalty is due not to a common source but to the commonality of the same revelation being experienced by various people in various cultures and at various times.

The Bardo itself might be compared to graduation time at the School of Life's year-end. Some 'souls', a minority, will graduate with honors and leave the school forever to attend their higher destiny. Most 'souls' will pass their examination to be reborn into a higher grade. Some will fail and have to repeat life until the required lessons are properly learnt. Some will fail so miserably that they will be put back to a more junior grade. A few will be expelled entirely.

The *Bardo Thödol* begins with the instructions to address the dead or dying as follows, "O nobly born —— (whatever the person's full name), listen! Now thou are experiencing the Radiance of the Clear Light of Pure Reality." By addressing the person as nobly born, his/her spiritual divinity is acknowledged first and foremost. Then the 'tour' of the Bardo begins. Typical of far eastern spiritual books, the best comes first. In descending order of desirability, the four stages of the Bardo are described. Briefly, these are:

<u>Stage 1</u> - The Clear Light. Enlightened beings with little or no help from a Lama go directly into Light and are liberated forever from the Karmic wheel of endless births and deaths. Like a stream hastening into the eternal ocean, the soul rapidly flows to merge into the One.

<u>Stage 2</u> - The Secondary Clear Light. With much guidance from a Lama and many prayers, an evolved person, one who has been a Seeker during his lifetime, may recognize the Clear Light and achieve Liberation. If, as commonly happens, the dead does not realize he is dead and is completely unaware of the Light, or if the pull of worldly charms is too great, then he quickly descends to the next lower stage.

<u>Stage 3</u> - The Dreaming Body. Here the deceased feels he is in a dream and has a dream-like body. First the Peaceful Deities appear. These are mental apparitions, related to the belief system held while alive—a Buddhist may see a Buddha seated on a golden lotus; a Christian may be greeted by Jesus or the Saints may lead him to the throne of God; or an ancient Egyptian may meet Osiris. With much help from the Lama, it is possible to surrender to these Deities and still achieve Liberation.

Next appear the Wrathful Deities which are also

products of the consciousness and related to the fears, angers, and stresses that one had in life. If, as these horrible creatures devour and torture, the deceased remembers he cannot die or be killed and that he is immortal and divine, Liberation is still possible. Usually, in terror, he tries to escape from these screaming, ghastly, blood-dripping demons and is chased down into the least attractive realm of the Bardo.

Stage 4 - The Intermediate State. This state of the Bardo is experienced before a rebirth. Here are those who ignored the opportunities that their life provided to seek enlightenment and were ignorant, oblivious to the true purpose of life. Here the deceased acquires a radiant body with special powers and limitations. He is very aware of the world, his funeral, the thoughts and deeds of his family and friends. If his past life was meritorious, pleasures, happiness, and ease will be experienced in this 'better' world with other radiant beings. If his past life was evil, demons will pursue and torture him, and the agonies of purgatory experienced. If his past life was one of neither evil nor merit, a colorless, dull, stupid indifference will be his.

Later comes Judgement Day where rebirth in a new body is assigned. It is also a psychological moment when it is possible with an exertion of will and the lama's guidance to repudiate anger, desire, possessiveness and embrace love and so obtain a good rebirth. The old body then grows dim and the new body grows more clear. Six *lokas* or rebirths are possible: an Angelic realm; a super birth in the world near an enlightened lama; a normal human birth; birth as a brute or animal; birth as vegetation; and finally, birth as a howling ghost in everlasting hell.

Today, many reports on the after-life have been made by people who "clinically died". They usually describe the after-life place like an idealized version of this planet. In a park-like setting radiant people welcome the new arrival. The similarity to the fourth stage of the Bardo is striking.

Infrequently, some people report that they saw Jesus or some other God-like figure surrounded by light and occassionally there are reports of meeting the Devil or his henchmen. These reports correspond nicely to the third Bardo stage.

Rare indeed are reports of dissolving into light, the higher Bardo stages. When discussing these higher stages some have said, "I don't want that to happen to me. I don't want to lose my individuality."

What is that "I" that does not want to lose itself? Is it not the ego? The Bardo holds a place for such as these. Merging into light in the higher stages is like a raindrop falling into the ocean. It loses its petty individuality and becomes the infinite ocean. As ocean, it still knows the raindrop as well as all other raindrops, all rivers, streams, fogs, ices, glaciers, and snows. Only the ego is lost. Everything else is gained.

A summary of the creed of the *Bardo Thödol* is that one's deeds in this life, one's merit, as well as one's beliefs, govern the Bardo experience. Furthermore, it explains that enlightenment and liberation are always right there for us and can be obtained in life, at the moment of death, or even after death, while in the Bardo.

In life, there are degrees of clarity in the experience of enlightenment, the clear light of the *Bardo Thödol*. Certainly this has been true in my lifetime—from my earliest dim experiences at the age of seven to my deeper, more profound and brighter revelations in later life. Of all these, no vision was more clear to me than the vision of my death and of what happened next.

After that precognition, I held the belief that my experience was what everyone else would also experience when they died. When I grew older and a little wiser, I changed my mind. Too often, in our Western culture we believe that if this is right then that *must* be wrong. We polarize our world into opposites. What grief this causes—arguments and fights with our mates and friends—labor and political strife—wars between nations. Often the Eastern culture is far richer—and the *Bardo Thödol* is a good example. Instead of believing this or that, the belief includes this and that. Instead of a narrow belief as to what will happen after death, it includes all possibilities, all evidence, and incorporates it into a unified belief system.

Inasmuch as I never questioned the truth and reality of my vision of the after-life, why should I doubt the reports of others' experiences just because they differ? Including all such experiences as truth and reality makes more sense as in the *Bardo Thödol*. I still believe, however, that what I experienced is what I will eventually experience personally.

Incidentally, that vision, which occurred in my mid-forties, has been proven true already, at least in one small detail. I saw myself as old and what hair remained was white. Now, almost a quarter of a century later, I am old and the hair remaining is quite white.

As I begin to describe what happened, the whole vision recurs once more, fresh and vivid. I had been listening to a recording of a symphony by Richard Straus. The music ended. Silence enveloped me. I experienced:

My Death

I am looking down at my body, several feet below me. It is old and shrunken. The tired, lined face has a waxy luminosity, the pallor of death. The breathing is shallow—uneven—it comes in small weak gasps. I am attached to my body by only a faint, tenuous silvery thread.

Covered by a coarse brown woollen blanket my body lies on a small bed or cot on one side of a large dimly lit room. Several people are present: a doctor, a nurse, and those dear ones I have so deeply loved. There is an unreal hush, for no one is certain what to do or say in the presence of death.

Someone is whispering——some faces are wet with tears——some mouths are tightly pressed——someone is weeping loudly and trying to control it——is it my first born, my oldest daughter? Her tears sound bitter; her cries grow louder, become sobs——she is led out of the room by another daughter. I wonder why she sobs so hard——but am too tired to even try to guess——I am too tired to think at all——it does not matter——nothing matters any more.

The pain had been bad, but now it is easier. It is still there but no longer of much importance——it is far away. Everything seems far away——I am apart——.

The dear ones I have loved, come close to me in turn. Some sit beside me for a moment in silence. Others whisper or say something——I hear the sound of their words but do not understand——it is not important. I wish to comfort them——I 'will' my arm to rise——I want to touch them, caress them——but the arm is too heavy and does not move.

I try to speak——to say everything's okay and that I love them——but no words come——I am too weak——helpless——exhausted——nothing really matters anyway. I am weary——so weary——tired——so very tired. I wish to sleep——a deep sleep——a final sleep. It's okay. It feels right——both life and death seem good——it's all as it should be——I am content.

The beat of my heart grows louder and louder, the sound reverberates and fills my ears——I listen——I wait——the body sleeps.

I drift away from the body——not far——too soon I am drawn back again. With effort, I open my eyes.

The room is darkened, quiet, empty——I am alone——I guess it is very late at night. I close my eyes——it seems brighter with my eyes closed. People, loved ones, places; the episodes of my life tumble and flash before me——not in a jumble and not in any order——I see it all like a single intricate tapestry——a completed tapestry——the weaving finished. There my parents——there I paddle a northern lake——there I am running paths through the bush——there the explorer, the oil company executive——there my lovers——there a school fight and crying in anger and shame at being beaten. Flash after flash comes——places I have been——long Arctic nights, the silence shattered as a tree explodes from the intense cold——shadowed jungles——I smell the humid decay——the prairies——the deserts——the mountains I climbed——Oh! you are *my* prairies, *my* deserts, *my* jungle, *my* mountains. I love you——I love you all! And there's my Cup of Life ——now lying on its side——how long ago it was offered——I have drunk well——the Cup is empty.

Other tapestries I briefly glimpse ——the designs my children weave and those newer looms with fewer strands that are my grandchildren's. How different from my own——and how exquisite. How dear they are——oh! my children——I love you——oh! so many loves——friends——I see you all—I love you——I love——all I have known, touched——all places——all things——all I am——I love you. I love you.

I have drifted away once more. Far off I hear sweet music——but not a melody of this world. I dimly see a light——but not the light of this world. I smell faint perfume——but not an aroma of this world. I sense a love——but a love beyond the understanding of this world.

I pause——I want to go further, but cannot——I want to penetrate the thin veil in front of me——I long to go into it——to submerge myself in it——I cannot——

I am still joined——the thin silver filament still holds me to the body.

Once more I am pulled back——but remain outside——I scan the body——the heart beat irregular——the breathing forced, jagged——how laborious to pull the air in——how easy to let it sigh out. The body is on automatic——I am not associated with it——I am barely attached.

Soaring——I rise——I fly in or out, I know not where——there are no directions here——I am in space and moving towards the Light.

I am pulled back yet once again. I touch the body——my tired, worn body that served me so well. I wait. It will be soon. One final inhalation. One final sigh. It is finished. I am free. Free of body, free of boundaries——free!

Suddenly my spirit knows with a profound certainty——I will not return to the world again. Not return? Not come this way again? How can I say good-bye? Not love my loves once more? Not hold a child to my breast again? Not hear laughter? Oh, such anguish! So much to touch, that I would touch once more. So much to do, that I would know once more. So much to see and hear, that I would have once more. So much to love, so much to love, so much I love.

The world revolves and floats near me in space. Overflowing with love, I fill the earth with love. I bathe it in love until it begins to glow with the light of love and the whole world and all within it becomes an expression of that love.

My love expands——swells and grows and increases beyond measure——and becomes transcendent, infinite. That Love is also Light——I am going into brighter and brighter Light!

I whisper a last good-bye to the earth I loved. No

need to return. The world is but a part of my becoming, a shining speck of stardust in an universe filled with love and light. The entire cosmos throbs——it is love——all love. And still I am flowing——rushing——into brighter and ever brighter Light——and further yet——beyond that——and beyond that——to where a Greater Light——a greater Glory shines. I go into it——I burst——I explode——Ecstacy!——I am that Light——I am That——I am——I AM!

About the Author

Bruce McDougall's first career included being an exploration geologist, geophysicist and executive in the oil industry. Over a period of 25 years, he worked on four continents for both major oil conglomerates and his own highly successful independent venture capital companies, making numerous discoveries of oil, gas and minerals.

A self-made millionaire, he retired from the oil industry in 1969, at the age of 48, to devote his full time and energy to the study of the potential for self-development we all possess. After spending a year in meditative solitude, he began a teaching career conducting courses in stress management at colleges, universities, private corporations and government agencies throughout western Canada.

In addition to conducting seminars and working as a lay counsellor for much of his life, he is the founder of the New Ventures Foundation, a Vancouver-based, non-profit organization devoted to the teaching of effective, successful living, as well as techniques such as meditation and stress management.

He has four children and ten grandchildren.